the economics of
competitive coexistence

COMMUNIST ECONOMIC STRATEGY:

The Rise of Mainland China

by

A. Doak Barnett

GREENWOOD PRESS, PUBLISHERS
WESTPORT, CONNECTICUT

Library of Congress Cataloging in Publication Data

Barnett, A   Doak.
   Communist economic strategy.

   Reprint of the ed. published by the National
Planning Association, Washington, in series: The
Economics of competitive coexistence.
   Includes bibliographical references.
   1. China--Economic policy. I. Title. II. Se-
ries: The Economics of competitive coexistence.
[HC427.9.B3 1975]   338.951   75-28661
ISBN 0-8371-8478-9

HC
427.9
B3
1975

CONTENTS

CONTENTS - 2

BACKGROUND

Ever since the Soviet bloc began its trade-and-aid drive in the un-committed countries of Asia and the Middle East under the slogan of "competitive coexistence," Western statesmen and economists have been pondering its implications. What is the impact in the less developed areas and the effect on world trade and production? What use is being made of the economic instrument in Soviet and in Western policy? How great is the capability of the Soviet bloc for a further expansion of these activities that cause so much concern in the West?

The study of the Economics of Competitive Coexistence was proposed by the NPA International Committee and set up in 1956 as a separate project to investigate these questions and a host of related problems. As an aid to its forthcoming general analysis, the project has had pre-pared a number of country and area studies, of which the present one on Mainland China is the fourth to reach the public. Together with its pre-viously published companion volume on East-Central Europe, and one in preparation on the Soviet Union, this report is designed to throw some light on the Sino-Soviet bloc's capabilities to maintain and expand its so-called trade-and-aid offensive, while striving to realize its other economic objectives, including rapid growth.

The Rockefeller Foundation in 1956 and 1957 made two grants to finance the NPA Project on the Economics of Competitive Coexistence. The Foundation is not, however, to be understood as approving by virtue of its grants any of the views expressed in research studies growing out of the project.

NPA is grateful for the Rockefeller Foundation's financial support and is deeply indebted to all who are contributors to this project: to the chair-man and the members of the Special Project Committee on the Economics of Competitive Coexistence; to the project's research staff; and especially to A. Doak Barnett, the author of the present study on <u>Communist Economic Strategy: The Rise of Mainland China</u>.

H. CHRISTIAN SONNE
Chairman, NPA Board of Trustees

STATEMENT

by the

NPA Special Project Committee on THE ECONOMICS OF COMPETITIVE COEXISTENCE

The rise of Communist China has been the outstanding development in Asia in recent years. The most populous nation in the world, Mainland China has been stampeded and cajoled, coerced and persuaded with single-mindedness of purpose into a social and intellectual conformity that few observers of earlier Chinese ways would have believed possible. While there are indications of discontent, this unprecedented transition took place in less than a decade and, so far at least, without major overt resistence.

The implications for the rest of the world, and particularly for Asia, are twofold. Some 650 million people, unified under a nationalistic, confident, purposeful, and ruthless leadership, would constitute an explosive charge of political power, even in the absence of a social message that is bound to affect many while others remain vigilant or fearful. Whether the force of attraction or the force of repulsion will eventually prevail is one crucial question. Another may well arise before the political effects of growing power have attained their full impact. Will less developed countries in Asia, and perhaps elsewhere, be attracted by the determined dynamism of the Chinese example? Might they be tempted by a rapid economic growth in China to try totalitarian methods, despite the evident cost in individual lives, freedom and dignity? Could sustained progress in Communist China eventually overshadow the sacrifice if perhaps, with time, the earliest measures were to be relaxed?

These are the long-range issues, but the test of time for the measurement of communist achievement lies still ahead. While the succession of developments has been rapid, and brash claims have been crowding each other in a relentless bid for world attention, uncontroversial facts are hard to come by. The Communists have completed their first plan, and the resulting increases in production appear to have been sizable, even if the official claims are treated with caution. A number of independent appraisals suggest that average growth in national product from 1952 to 1957 was hardly less than 6 to 7 percent per annum, and it may well have been more.

In 1958 the Chinese Communists announced a drastic "leap forward;" their targets and subsequent claims of achievement have lately defied belief. Under this barrage of propaganda, it may be tempting to take shelter in healthy skepticism of any and all claims until corroboration. Yet, foreign observers and experts, accustomed to piece together scattered bits of evidence, seem inclined to believe in a measure of acceleration resulting from an unprecedented mobilization of human resources. Literally millions are put to work on large-scale public works; women have been "freed" from housework through the establishment of eating-halls and nurseries in the newly created people's communes, the semimilitary social organization that has recently blanketed the Chinese countryside; and everyone, intellectual, party-worker, or working-man, "voluntarily" devotes spare time to the tasks of the moment -- harvest, manure-making, or backyard furnaces -- to the limit of physical endurance.

Such massive efforts are bound to have some results in additional output, at least in the short run. Where productivity and yields had been low, it stands to reason that purpose, drive, and huge injections of human capital can achieve a good deal, even though claims for miracles need not be accepted In fact, if the Communists could overcome the ageless stagnation in Chinese agriculture, as they claim to be doing, and continue to extract long hours of arduous labor while keeping consumption down, they might even be confident of solving the problem of their rapid increase of population. It is revealing that an earlier drive for birth control has quietly lapsed and that a growing population is now viewed as an asset, rather than a deterrent, to economic growth.

For all the recent stress of small-scale industry, the Chinese Communists have pushed ahead with hundreds of large projects. Even though they are now making more of their own equipment, they remain dependent on the Soviet bloc for much of their machinery and technical know-how. But, in spite of never-failing protestations of solidarity, there is evidence that these vital imports remain subject to hard bargaining; and Soviet credits, as distinct from technical assistance, have been anything but generous. Most imports have to be paid by Chinese exports, including foods that are rationed at home. It is significant that China's trade balance with the Soviet Union has been positive over the past several years, probably in repayment of past loans, perhaps including military assistance rendered during the Korean War. Nonetheless, even though capital exports to China have been relatively modest, the supply of development goods on such a large scale did not come about without any effort within the bloc. While this may strain some capital goods industries and perhaps diminish temporarily Soviet capabilities at home and elsewhere, imports from China satisfy needs within the bloc, or can be re-exported with telling effect, as with Chinese tin.

Even though trade with the Soviet bloc is under the circumstances the mainstay of Chinese foreign economic relations, trade with noncommunist countries has also increased steeply. Both the volume and the composition of this trade have assumed economic and political significance. Mainland China has frequently appeared as a buyer of goods primary producers found difficult to sell in world markets: rubber, cotton, and even rice of which it has become a major exporter at the same time. More importantly, the Communists are using their growing industry to sell consumer goods (and even some capital goods) on a rising scale, including cotton textiles that are rationed at home. These sales, priced to win against any competition, have become a major concern to other exporters to Southeast. Asia, including India and Japan. Although the Chinese undoubtedly need foreign exchange badly to pay for their growing imports, their export drive is hardly devoid of political intent as well. Especially in the case of Japan, a desire to hurt through competition fits in well with the stoppage of direct trade relations by China that followed political disagreements in which both "stick and carrot" were prominently featured by the Communists. And, with emphasis on the "carrot," Communist China has been giving loans and grants to a number of less developed countries, despite its own strained balance of payments.

The significance of the problems of growth and those of trade are discussed in the present study and the NPA Special Project Committee on The Economics of Competitive Coexistence believes that <u>Communist Economic Strategy: The Rise of Mainland China</u> by A. Doak Barnett is a valuable contribution to a field in which knowledge has so far been limited. Without endorsing details, for which the author, in collaboration with the director of research, assumes responsibility, and without subscribing necessarily to all interpretations and policy implications suggested by the study, the Committee recommends to the NPA Board of Trustees publication of this timely study.

Members of the NPA Special Project Committee
on THE ECONOMICS OF COMPETITIVE COEXISTENCE
Signing the Statement

SIMON KUZNETS (Chairman)
Professor of Political Economy
Johns Hopkins University

JOHN H. ADLER
Economic Advisor
International Bank for
Reconstruction and Development

FRANK ALTSCHUL
Chairman of the Board
General American
Investors Company

SOLOMON BARKIN
Director of Research
Textile Workers Union
of America, AFL-CIO

AUGUST HECKSCHER
Director
The Twentieth Century Fund

STRUVE HENSEL
Attorney
Washington, D. C.

STACY MAY
International Basic
Economy Corporation

MAX F. MILLIKAN
Director
Center for International
Studies
Massachusetts Institute
of Technology

ARTHUR MOORE
The Washington Bureau
McGraw-Hill Publications

PHILIP E. MOSELY
Director of Studies
Council on Foreign Relations

PAUL H. NITZE
President
Foreign Service
Educational Foundation

H. CHRISTIAN SONNE
President
South Ridge Corporation

FOREWORD

This study of Communist China is the second of three studies on Communist economic strategy which investigate the capabilities of the Sino-Soviet bloc in the struggle known as "competitive coexistence." While the importance of the East-Central European countries has been overshadowed by the dominant position of the Soviet Union, the emerging place of China in the Communist bloc is unmistakable. Indeed, its harsh voice has of late become so loud that some observers have begun to wonder who was leading whom in theory and in practice. At present, the pre-eminence of the Soviet Union within the bloc has been reconfirmed, and undoubtedly China remains dependent on the Soviet Union for much of its imports for development purposes. But Mao's China has repeatedly asserted itself with unexpected vigor, and as its economic strength increases, the weight of China's 650 million people and its ageless national pride may well be felt more decisively.

In the meantime, the shadow of Communist China upon Asia is lengthening visibly. If "competitive coexistence" is seen to manifest itself largely in the fields of trade, aid, and development performance, the role of China is vividly evident in all three. While, compared with the West, China is still a small trader in most of Asia, it has made its intrusion effective far beyond its proportionate share, both as a buyer of burdensome surpluses and as a determined seller to the discomfiture of other Asian producers, not to mention those in the West. And this is perhaps only the beginning. As China's industrial capacity grows, along with its need for imports and the wherewithal to pay for them, this drive may well be intensified.

Domestic needs have never been allowed to prevail over economically or politically motivated exports. While the distinction between these motivations is sometimes blurred, there can be no doubt about the reason for giving grants and loans -- more grants, in fact, than the wealthier Soviet Union has ever extended. Invariably this financial assistance has gone to small neutralist countries, most of them in the Southeast Asian area, that may well form the arc of China's closest ambitions, but even extending to the Near East. That this can be done at all while China is straining mercilessly for development at home, is in itself apt to be seen as a token of strength. Further, while the Soviet Union likes to pose as an Asian power, there can be no doubt where China's influence begins. And Chinese residents and institutions in other Asian countries are being openly and boldly enlisted for the "motherland's" political cause.

While it is too early to evaluate the eventual impact of these moves on the uncommitted countries, one should already note the energy and drive they symbolize. This self-confidence is rooted in the achievements the Communists have claimed for their development at home. No attempt is made to disguise the harshness of sacrifice that is involved in mass efforts unparalleled in modern history. On the contrary, the self-denial of any individuality in joint endeavors is pushed to the limit; and while this is bound to cause resentment, foreign observers have also noticed a measure of willingness, even some enthusiasm, without which no revolution could have been carried to such a degree of social experimentation. And whether one believes in the eventual futility of this effort or not, the West would do well to recognize the strength of the revolutionary impetus that is at work.

To what extent this example will affect other Asian countries remains to be seen. Much will depend on the capability of the Chinese Communists for sustained achievement, rather than spasms of supreme effort such as are now in evidence. But even during China's first Five Year Plan, afflicted by much bad planning along with assorted natural disasters, growth seems to have proceeded at higher total and per capita rates than in any other undeveloped Asian country, perhaps twice as high as in India, where the longing for development, and the need for it, are equally great. It is noteworthy, though, that Japan has done as well as China, at least until the recent recession began. Whether the totalitarian example of China will prove more attractive than the system that has proved itself in Japan and, of course, in the West, is a most crucial problem for the future. Thus, the course of Communist China -- its successes or failures -- is a decisive element.

To report on the tortuous course of development in Communist China requires an intimate knowledge of the sources and an ability to interpret them critically. The Project on the Economics of Competitive Coexistence was happy to engage Mr. A. Doak Barnett, an expert in the field, to undertake this study. Mr. Barnett was born and raised in China where he returned again in 1947 after studies at Yale University. After two years in China (including eight months under Communist rule) as an Associate of the Institute of Current World Affairs and correspondent for the Chicago Daily News he served as a consultant to the Economic Cooperation Administration, member of the U. S. Foreign Service, and Associate of the American Universities Field Staff in Hong Kong. Lately, he has been Head of the Department of Area Studies, Foreign Service Institute, and a Research Fellow of the Council on Foreign Relations.

In addition to the unfailing assistance and advice of Dr. Gerhard Colm, NPA Chief Economist, the project staff and the author are indebted to many persons too numerous to list. However, for their uncommon contribution of time and effort in the form of comments and criticism of an earlier version of the manuscript, special thanks are due to Alexander Eckstein, Feng-hwa Mah, Paul Wohl, Carl Remer, Sidney Klein, H. D. Fong, Edwin Jones and William W. Hollister. This acknowledgement is, however, not intended to imply any responsibility on the part of such persons for the conclusions or opinions expressed by the author in this study.

With few exceptions, only data and information available to the writer by March 1, 1959, could be considered in this study. In a field where developments sometimes follow each other in rapid sequence, this cautionary note seems well worth bearing in mind.

Henry G. Aubrey, Director of Research
The Economics of Competitive Coexistence

COMMUNIST ECONOMIC STRATEGY:

THE RISE OF MAINLAND CHINA

by

A. Doak Barnett

INTRODUCTION

Since the establishment of the Peking government in 1949, the Chinese Communist regime has dedicated itself to the achievement of rapid industrialization and world power status. Communist China's leaders have shaped both their domestic and foreign policies to these ends, and Peking has in recent years assumed a role of steadily increasing importance in economic competition between the Communist bloc and the West.

The high degree of totalitarian political power possessed by Mao Tse-tung and his colleagues has enabled the Peking regime to mobilize the manpower and resources of China for domestic economic development in a manner impossible for past Chinese governments. The Chinese Communists, using the Soviet Union as a general model but experimenting also with new approaches and methods, have proceeded to socialize China's economy and to initiate an extraordinarily ambitious program of industrial expansion.

As a result, Communist China's economic position has undergone fundamental changes during the past nine years. The institutional basis for economic life in China has been completely reshaped. The wealth of the country has been ruthlessly redistributed and brought under effective government control. By keeping living standards close to the minimum required for subsistence, the Chinese Communists have been able -- as the national income has risen -- to achieve an unprecedented rate of national saving and investment and, consequently, to initiate an impressive program of economic growth.

The focus of this program has been upon industrialization. Particularly since the start of China's first Five Year Plan in 1953, the Chinese Communists have been rapidly and energetically building China's industrial base, concentrating primarily upon heavy industries, and they have made significant progress. During the last year of the first Five Year Plan, 1957, the stresses and strains created by the industrialization program began to make themselves increasingly felt in China, but Peking's leaders decided to push ahead in their development program as rapidly as possible nonetheless, and in 1958 they announced a dramatic "great leap forward" and embarked upon audacious programs to "communize" the peasants and to develop decentralized small-scale industries.

Basic changes in China's foreign economic relations have accompanied these domestic developments. Upon achieving power, the Chinese Communists not only aligned themselves immediately with the Soviet Union in a political sense, but they also proceeded to reorient China's foreign economic relations

Note: All footnotes appear on page 102 ff.

1

away from the West and toward the Soviet bloc. In the past nine years, as industrialization has developed within China, the level of Communist China's foreign trade has steadily risen, and the Chinese Communists' capabilities of conducting an active foreign economic policy have been enhanced significantly.

Recently, the Chinese Communists have become increasingly involved in the economic competition which has developed between the two major power blocs. For reasons which are clearly political as well as economic, Peking has actively fostered trade relations with the non-Communist world, and it is now playing a major role in Communist bloc trading with countries in the Asian-African area. Within the past two years, furthermore, Communist China has initiated several small but significant foreign aid programs to non-Communist Asian countries. And, surprising as it may seem, the Chinese Communists by 1956 appeared to have become net capital exporters, despite the fact that they were still in the early stages of their own development.

These recent developments have taken place within the context of basic changes in Communist China's overall foreign policy and in the entire Soviet bloc's approach to competition with the West. Even before the fighting in Korea was brought to a halt by the truce signed in 1953, Peking's leaders, following Moscow's lead, began to shift from a bellicose emphasis upon threat and subversion to a policy of extending their influence by fostering closer relations with the non-Communist countries of the Asian-African area and encouraging neutralism under the banner of the "five principles of coexistence." During this period, the entire Communist bloc, including Communist China, consciously embarked upon a policy of economic competition with the West and began steadily increasing its use of trade, aid, and other components of economic policy as major instruments of overall policy.

The changes during the past nine years in Communist China's economic position, and the significant role which Peking is now playing in international economic affairs, pose many basic questions which need to be answered if the future of competition between the Communist bloc and the West is to be adequately understood in the West.

What is the rate of economic growth now taking place in Communist China, and what have the Chinese Communists actually achieved since the start of their first Five Year Plan? What are the major domestic economic problems now facing Peking? Is it likely that despite existing problems, Communist China will continue to make rapid progress in its program of industrialization?

Is it likely that population pressure and food scarcity will eventually force China into a pattern of stagnation? Or is it possible that Communist China will be able to make sustained economic progress? To what degree are the Chinese Communists economically dependent upon the Soviet Union, and does Communist China constitute a significant drain on the Soviet bloc? Or is Peking, despite its economic dependence in many respects upon the Soviet bloc, capable of making an important contribution to the bloc and to overall bloc policies of competition with the West?

What is the economic and competitive potential of Communist China in relation to Southeast Asia and to Japan? To what extent is it likely that the Chinese Communists will make their economic influence increasingly felt in Southeast Asia?

What "demonstration effect" will Communist China have upon the underdeveloped areas of the world if it continues to build up its heavy industry at a rapid rate? Is there a possibility that Asian nations will be significantly impressed and influenced by the Chinese model, despite the costs of totalitarian rule and economic hardship in Communist China, if their own economies do not grow at a rate comparable to the rate of growth in China? Will China be able, as Peking hopes, to exert a power of attraction on other underdeveloped countries?

In broad terms, a competitive struggle of great long-run significance is now underway in the underdeveloped areas of the world. Communist China, as the largest and strongest Communist country in Asia, and as the most important ally of the Soviet Union, is a major participant in the competition. A realistic appraisal of Communist China's economic capabilities, its foreign economic policies, and its potential impact on other underdeveloped nations is therefore essential to any general assessment of the world-wide economic competition now going on between the Communist bloc and the West.

PART I

COMMUNIST CHINA'S DOMESTIC ECONOMY

Chapter One

THE ECONOMIC BASE

When the Chinese Communists came to power in 1949, they inherited an underdeveloped economy which had been badly disrupted by years of war, inflation, and weak government.

Although the West had a profound impact upon China from the mid-19th century onwards, modern industry was still in its infancy at the time of Communist takeover. Roughly four fifths of China's huge population was engaged in farming or in occupations closely related to agriculture. Methods of cultivation were intensive, but modern scientific techniques of farming were almost unknown to the average peasant. Output per acre was fairly high by Asian standards (outside Japan) but output per man was low and agriculture barely supported subsistence standards of life for the mass of the peasantry.

Since about the 17th century, the population in China has grown rapidly, and the Chinese suffered from a severe land shortage. The majority of the good arable land was cultivated, and the total cultivated land in the country amounted to only about one half an acre per person. The economic and social ill-effects of small and fragmented landholdings were multiplied by the prevalence of landlordism and tenancy. And, although Chinese governments had through the centuries devoted considerable attention to water conservation, the Chinese peasants continued to be plagued by droughts, periodic floods, and famines.

These and many other factors had traditionally kept the living standards of the Chinese rural population close to the subsistence level. In the 19th century and early 20th century, the situation of the peasants further deteriorated due to population growth, ineffective government, civil disturbances, the decay of rural handicrafts in competition with manufactured goods, and the deterioration of existing water conservation works. In the early 1930s, the Chinese Nationalist government made efforts to halt this process, but its programs were interrupted by the war with Japan, which caused agricultural output to decline to a new low, and by the subsequent Nationalist-Communist conflict, which delayed restoration of output to the prewar 1936 level.

Modern industry in China before the Communist takeover was limited in extent and very localized. Most of it had been developed by foreigners -- among whom the British and Japanese played leading roles -- and except for the heavy industry in Manchuria which the Japanese developed and controlled between 1931 and 1945, most industrial output in China consisted of consumer goods, such as cotton textiles. Existing factories were concentrated for the most part in a few coastal "treaty ports" where foreign capital and ownership predominated. The region around Shanghai was the most important center of light industry and produced the bulk of the country's consumer goods. Secondary centers of considerable importance included the Peking-Chinwangtao-Tientsin region, the Shantung area between Tsingtao and Tsinan, a Central China area around Wuhan, and the Pearl River delta at Canton.

The only significant heavy industrial base in China was the one fostered by the Japanese during the 1930s in the Anshan-Fushun-Mukden area of Manchuria. During the period of Japanese rule, investment in Manchuria in modern industry and transport was greatly expanded. In rough terms, it is estimated that such investment increased from $1 billion to $5 billion (in 1945 dollars) between 1936 and 1945, although various shortages and imbalances prevented the new plant capacity from coming into full production. Despite deterioration and Soviet looting in 1945-46, the remaining Japanese-built plant capacity in Manchuria, when later rehabilitated and brought into full production by the Chinese Communists, was to be largely responsible for the rapid growth in industrial output during the first years of Communist rule. Industries in Manchuria included iron and steel plants, power plants, coal mines, and metallurgical factories, and these were supported by the best railway net in China.

Even when prewar industrial production was at its peak, China was by almost any standard one of the least industrialized of all major nations. One symbolic indicator of this was the fact that steel production never reached the level of one million tons a year (see Appendix Table 5 for the present Peking regime's estimates of peak production figures prior to Communist takeover). Furthermore, the industry which did exist had declined as a result of the war with Japan and its aftermath. Industry in the "treaty ports," which had passed into Japanese hands during the war and had subsequently been taken over for the most part by the Nationalist government, was seriously affected by the inflation and disruption of conditions caused by the Communist-Nationalist civil war. Industry in Manchuria was crippled by the Soviet removals of equipment as war booty and the destruction of equipment by looters, which took place in 1945. The postwar Pauley Commission reported in 1946 that Soviet removals and other damage to Manchuria's industries totaled between $850 million and $900 million and reduced productive capacity by one half in iron and steel and by sizable percentages in almost all industries.

Even before the war, China's industrial plant was not generally employed at peak capacity levels, and the attrition of war and political instability was such that at the time of the Communist takeover in 1949, China's limited industrial plant was producing well below prewar levels. The Communists claimed that compared with previous peak levels of output, production in 1949 had declined by 80 to 90 percent in steel, 50 percent in cement, and between 10 and 30 percent in the most important consumer goods.

In economic terms, the first task facing the Chinese Communists after 1949, therefore, was the achievement of economic stability and the restoration of existing productive capacity. By stringent fiscal and financial measures they were able to halt inflation. The establishment of unified political control, the repair of transportation, and the renewal of domestic trade assisted the recovery of both agricultural and industrial output during the 1949-52 period, which the Chinese Communists now label as the "period of restoration."

However, there were also serious disrupting influences on the Chinese economy during this period, including the violent redistribution of land under Peking's "agrarian reform" program, and the numerous revolutionary mass campaigns conducted by the Communists such as the campaign against counterrevolutionaries and the "Three Anti and Five Anti" campaigns -- the latter was a bitter attack against "five evils," including tax evasion and corruption, attributed to the business class.

Major strains were imposed upon the Chinese economy also by the Korean War and other military activities. Despite these stresses, however, economic output did climb toward prewar levels. By 1952, the Chinese Communists claimed that overall industrial production in 33 major products had risen 26 percent above previous peak levels -- 16 percent in capital goods and 32 percent in consumer goods. Specifically, they stated, for example, that production of steel, cotton yarn, and some other major products was over two fifths higher than past record levels (see Appendix Table 5). The claim that prewar output levels had been achieved by 1952 was an exaggeration, but by the end of 1952 the Chinese Communists were ready to embark upon a program of industrial expansion and to make preparations for their first Five Year Plan.

Chapter Two

THE FIRST FIVE YEAR PLAN-- OVERALL
PATTERN OF ECONOMIC DEVELOPMENT 1/

The Chinese Communists' drive to build modern industrial power took concrete form in their first Five Year Plan which was initiated at the start of 1953. During the years 1953-57, fulfillment of this Plan became the primary focus of national life in Communist China. The plans and claimed achievements of this five year period are the key, therefore, to the Chinese Communists' economic development program during its initial phase, and they reveal both the overall pattern and the pace of the program.

As early as 1950, Peking indicated its determination to formulate a long-range development program. Preliminary steps toward evolving an overall economic plan started as early as 1951, and in 1952 the Chinese Communists outlined their twin goals of "socialization and industrialization" in a general statement of policy labeled "the general line of the State for a period of transition to socialism." When the first Five Year Plan officially got underway in 1953, however, the Peking regime still had no detailed long-range plans, and the regime proceeded with a series of one year plans.

It was not until mid-1955 -- after the signing of a truce in Korea and the conclusion of an aid agreement with the USSR, and after the Plan period was half completed -- that Peking publicly revealed the detailed targets of the first Five Year Plan. Shortly after publication of the Plan, furthermore, Mao Tse-tung called for rapid collectivization and better economic planning; the economic timetable was subsequently revised, so that in fact the first Five Year Plan reflected official thinking for only a brief period and served only a limited planning function. Nonetheless, the Plan targets as published in 1955 (see Appendix Table 2) reveal in general terms the economic objectives of the regime at that time.

In mid-1955, the Chinese Communists asserted that they expected to fulfill the "fundamental task of the transition period" in three Five Year Plan periods. By this they meant that they hoped to have completely socialized China's economy and to have constructed a significant industrial base by 1967. At the same time they recognized that industrialization in any full sense would require a much longer period, and that it would be 40 to 50 years before China could become "a powerful country with a high degree of socialist industrialization." The first Five Year Plan was to be the initial step on the long road to industrialization. It was clearly patterned on the Soviet model in its basic approach.

Although the Chinese Communists introduced significant innovations in their specific methods and timetable for socializing China's economy, they accepted with few, if any, major reservations the Soviet conception of rapid, forced industrialization, under state direction and control. The Soviet Union was explicitly proclaimed to be the model for China, and the Peking regime adopted slogans such as "the Soviet Union of today is the

7

China of tomorrow." China's first Five Year Plan, therefore, outlined a program focusing upon the rapid build-up of heavy industries as a base for industrial power and national strength, rather than upon raising living standards or improving welfare. It did, however, call for an impressive rate of overall economic growth.

The investment program for the first Five Year Plan, as revealed in mid-1955, is perhaps the clearest indication of the Chinese Communists' scale of priorities in economic development (see Appendix Tables 3 and 4). According to the Plan, the budgetary outlay during 1953-57 included investments in "capital construction" exceeding $18 billion during the five years, thus averaging over $3 billion annually. 2/ The "capital construction" investments were to be weighted heavily in favor of industrial development (see Appendix Table 3); 58.2 percent of all such investments was allocated for industry, and of this amount 88.8 percent ($9.3 billion) was to go to heavy industry and 11.2 percent ($1.2 billion) to light industry. By contrast, only 7.6 percent ($1.4 billion) of "capital construction" funds was earmarked for agriculture, forestry, and water conservation. Although the Plan revealed the Peking regime to be basically "industry-minded," considerable efforts were to be made in agriculture, in organizing experimental farms, extension services, data collection, and cadre-training; in mobilizing unpaid or low-paid farm labor for irrigation and similar improvement projects; and in mobilizing the peasants' own savings and investments.

This concentration upon industrial development was also revealed in the breakdown of specific construction projects scheduled under the first Five Year Plan as of mid-1955. The Plan called for initiation of over 7,600 construction projects, many of them entirely new enterprises but some merely additions to existing plant -- of these, 1,600 were to be the large-scale, so-called "above-norm" projects. 3/ Planned projects in the field of industry accounted for 694 of the "above-norm" projects, whereas only 252 were in the field of agriculture, forestry, and water conservation.

The general targets which the Chinese set for themselves, particularly those for gross output and industrial output, were very ambitious. The accent on industrialization is quite evident from the figures in Table 1.

Table 1

Selected Planned Rates of Growth, First Five Year Plan

	Total % increase 1952-57	Annual % rate of increase
Gross industrial and agricultural output	51.1	8.6
"Modern" industrial output	104.1	15.3
All industry (including handicrafts)	98.3	14.7
Agricultural output	23.3	4.3
Light industry output	79.7	12.4
Heavy industry output	126.5	17.8

From 1953 through 1957, the Chinese Communist regime struggled to achieve the economic goals which they had set for the country in the Five Year Plan. In human terms, their program involved one austerity program after another. Peking's leaders attempted to justify the necessary sacrifice on the part of the population by asserting that the "small betterment of today must be subordinated to the big betterment of tomorrow." In economic terms, the program involved continuous and severe strain on the limited resources of the nation.

By the end of 1957 it was clear, however, that in general terms the Peking regime had been able to achieve many of the overall objectives of the first Five Year Plan, and that it had exceeded numerous goals in the field of industrial development. The costs to the Chinese people of Peking's achievements were high. There had been some serious failures in the first Plan period; and in 1957, the final year of the Plan period, the Communists encountered many economic problems which created a stringent economic situation in China. But despite all difficulties, the Peking regime clearly had made notable progress in the field of heavy industry and had achieved an impressive rate of economic growth between 1953 and 1957.

The Chinese Communists now claim that the gross output of industry and agriculture rose more than 60 percent during the first Plan period (see Table 2). Modern industrial output, they assert, increased by about 133 percent -- over 200 percent in capital goods and 85 percent in consumer goods -- while the gross output of all industry including handicrafts is said to have increased by close to 120 percent. And gross agricultural production is claimed to have risen by almost 25 percent.

The problem of translating Peking's official figures into terms meaningful in the West is a complex one, since Communist China -- like the Soviet Union -- bases its statistics concerning output and national income on concepts different from those currently used in the West. Output figures such as those cited above, for example, are gross figures which do not take account of duplication between different industries and sectors of the economy, whereas in the West national income analysis is generally based upon net computations. Additional complications arise from the fact that the Chinese Communists, in line with Soviet practice, exclude from their national income estimates many services which Western economists include and there are other conceptual and definitional differences (see the Annex to this chapter on the use of Chinese Communist statistics).

However, it is possible for Western economists to gather data from varied official Chinese Communist sources, cross-check them for consistency to some extent, and then make independent estimates of Gross National Product (GNP), investments, and consumption in China using the criteria and methods accepted in the West. At present, a number of specialists in the United States are working on this problem, and some of the results of their efforts have already been published. The most ambitious attempt that has appeared to date is a study by the American specialist William W. Hollister. 4/ Hollister estimates that the rate of growth in Communist China's GNP during Peking's first Plan period was 11.0 percent if computed in current prices, or 8.6 percent if computed in constant 1952 prices. However, in an underdeveloped country such as China where producers' goods are often overpriced in relative terms, and are

9

steadily becoming more important in the economy as a whole, this can produce an upward bias which distorts the GNP estimates somewhat. Perhaps these GNP estimates should be slightly discounted, therefore, to take account of this fact. 5/ Even if this is done, however, Hollister's estimates would suggest that Communist China's GNP, in constant 1952 prices, increased during the first Plan period at an average rate of perhaps 7 to 8 percent per year, while the rate of per capita GNP growth during the period may have been close to 5 to 6 percent annually.

T. C. Liu's findings (based on research at the Rand Corporation) on the Chinese Communist economy during 1952-57 have resulted in estimates which, although slightly lower than Hollister's, are nonetheless comparable. Liu estimates that during its first Plan period, Communist China's average annual increase in net domestic product, expressed in 1952 prices, was 6.9 percent.

It is clear, therefore, that Communist China's rate of growth of about 7 to 8 percent during its first Plan period was impressive. It was substantially above that of most other underdeveloped countries. Significantly, it was much higher than India's rate of growth during its first five year plan. If Hollister's estimate of 8.6 percent is accepted, Communist China's rate of growth was over double the 4.0 percent achieved by India during 1951-56 (see Table 3).

However, Japan's case indicates that non-Communist Asian countries are also capable of achieving rapid economic growth, without resorting to the Communists' totalitarian methods. Japan's real national income during the 1950-56 period increased by an average of 8.6 percent annually, a rate of growth comparable to Communist China's. Japan achieved this rate despite the fact that it is already highly industrialized, and that generally growth rates decline in the more advanced stages of industrialization. This should not, however, obscure the significance of the fact that Communist China currently appears to be outstripping the underdeveloped, non-Communist Asian nations in the struggle for rapid economic development.

There are numerous explanations for Communist China's rapid rate of growth. One of the most fundamental is the high rate of investment which Peking has maintained. Hollister estimates that gross domestic investment in Communist China increased by an annual average of 19.6 percent, in 1952 prices, during 1952-57; and that as a percentage of GNP it increased from 9 percent in 1950 to 14.9 percent in 1952, to 17.8 percent in 1954, dropped to 15.8 percent in 1956, and then rose by almost one third to 20 percent in 1957. 6/ The investment spurt in 1957, a large part of which went into inventories, undoubtedly helped lay the groundwork for the "great leap forward" claimed in 1958. It should be noted that apart from building up inventories, state investment actually declined in 1957; in 1956 the Chinese drew heavily on stocks.

A high rate of investment is not the only explanation for Communist China's rapid economic growth, however. Another basic factor has been increased productivity and increased utilization of existing facilities, resulting both from technical improvements and from totalitarian methods which can exact maximum efforts from a controlled population. Actually, the incremental capital-output ratio--that is, the relationship between the investments made and the resulting increases in output--has been relatively low in Communist China.

10

Table 2

Annual Growth Rates of National Income, Investment and Consumption
1952-57 (First Plan)

	Percent
Gross National Product, a/ total	
Current prices	11.0
1952 prices	8.6
Gross National Product, per capita b/	
1952 prices	6.3
Gross Domestic Investment	
Current prices	17.7
1952 prices	19.6
Consumption, private and public c/	
Current prices	9.2
1952 prices	5.8
Consumption, private and public, per capita	
1952 prices b/	3.5
Personal Consumption c/	
1952 prices	6.2
Personal Consumption, per capita	
1952 prices	3.9

a/ In this figure for GNP, based on American concepts, all other services used in Western concepts had to be derived indirectly or imputed; and in this method there is a considerable margin of error. The 1957 figures were estimated by Hollister from preliminary rather than final figures, which, however, differ little from those used in his computations.

b/ An increase of population of 11.6 percent during the first Five Year Plan, or 2.2 percent per annum, was used for the computations in this table (for annual population estimates see Appendix Table 1). These figures therefore differ slightly from Hollister's own computation of GNP per capita, because he used a hypothetical population increase of 2 percent per annum.

c/ Consumption includes personal consumption (including farm home consumption, imputed house rent, and consumer services), and government purchases of goods and services. Personal consumption is shown separately in the table.

Source: William W. Hollister, op. cit., pp. 132-3.

Table 3

Annual Growth Rates of National Income in Constant Prices:
Mainland China, Japan, and India
(selected periods)

	Growth: percent p.a.	
	aggregate	per capita
China: 1952/57 (First Plan)	8.6	6.3
Japan: Real National Income (base 1950), 1950/56	8.6	6.4
India: GNP in 1952 prices, 1951/56 (First Plan)	4.0	2.6

Sources: China, see Table 2; Japan, Jerome B. Cohen, Japan's Postwar Economy, Bloomington, 1958, Table IV-1, p. 45; India, Wilfred Malenbaum, "India and China: Contrasts in Development Performance," American Economic Review, June 1959.

If one compares total investment during the first Plan period with claimed increases in output during those five years, the resulting incremental capital-output ratio is 2.5/1. 7/ Actually, if 1951-56 investment figures were compared with 1952-57 output figures, assuming a time lag between investment and its effects upon production, the incremental capital-output ratio would be even lower. All of this confirms in statistical terms what numerous visitors to Communist China have been able to observe -- namely that by imposing harsh totalitarian discipline upon its population and demanding extremely hard work from its labor force, Peking has obtained very high output increases from the investments it has made.

Increases in consumption have inevitably lagged behind the growth of national income in Communist China since investment has steadily taken an increasing share of total output. Hollister estimates that during the entire first Plan period, consumption (including both personal consumption and government purchases of goods and services) increased by an average of 5.8 percent annually, if computed in 1952 prices. According to Hollister's calculation, consumption (again including both private and public), as a percentage of GNP, fell from 90.7 percent in 1950, to 86.5 percent in 1952, and to 82.6 percent in 1954, then rose to 83.9 percent in 1956. However, in 1957 when investment rose, consumption dropped to 79.6 percent of GNP, 8/ even though in absolute terms it remained unchanged in 1952 prices and rose slightly in terms of current prices.

It is particularly difficult to make estimates of personal consumption in Communist China on the basis of official data, but Hollister has made an attempt to do so. His figures indicate that during the first Plan period personal consumption, as a percentage of GNP, dropped steadily from 79.8 percent in 1950 to 72.8 percent in 1956, and to 69.8 percent in 1957. Nonetheless, he estimates that average per capita personal consumption in Communist China increased at the not unimpressive annual rate of about 4 percent during the Plan period. 9/ However, T. C. Liu's study (which computes net rather than gross product) indicates that personal consumption grew less rapidly and accounted for a smaller share of net product than Hollister's estimates would suggest, while his estimates for both the rate of growth of government expenditures and their share of net product are higher than Hollister's.

Several qualifications or reservations must be made about any such estimate. A large part of the statistical rise may have resulted from the shift of population from rural to urban centers where more processing of food, and the like, is required, and costs of living are higher. In any case, there is no disputing the fact that despite the statistical rise in consumption suggested by overall national figures, substantial evidence has existed indicating consumer discontent in China. Consumers have faced disheartening queues and severe shortages of basic commodities in recent years. It is questionable, therefore, whether the statistical indications of increased consumption actually represent a significant improvement in welfare during the first Plan period.

Turning to income and living standards, the condition of some groups in China, such as urban workers, may have improved somewhat. The

Five Year Plan scheduled a 33 percent increase in workers' and employees' wages, and in late 1957 Peking asserted that the actual increase over the five years had been 37 percent. Premier Chou En-lai made the claim that workers' and employees' average wages had risen from $188 in 1952 to $258 in 1956; these figures refer to monetary wages rather than real wages. The peasantry -- the bulk of the population -- fared less well, however. Although in 1957 Peking claimed that peasants' incomes had increased 10.7 percent -- or 2.6 percent a year in the previous four years (a claim which is probably exaggerated) -- Chou En-lai stated that in 1956, average peasant incomes in all of China amounted to only $30 per peasant, and $127 per peasant household. At the same time he revealed that between 1952 and 1956, the volume of consumer goods output made available to the entire Chinese population had increased by an average of only $1.69 per person annually. Consumption and living standards were clearly given a relatively low priority in the Chinese Communists' economic development program, and the rapid rate of economic growth did not result in a rapid improvement in welfare of the population during the first Five Year Plan.

By the end of 1957, despite year-to-year fluctuations during the first Five Year Plan period in many of the basic indices of investment and growth in China, a general pattern had emerged which the Chinese Communists hoped to continue and to project into the second Five Year Plan period. This pattern called for a continued high rate of investment and industrial development. Peking asserted that in the five years ahead it hoped once again to raise national income by about 50 percent, maintaining an annual rate of increase of close to 9 percent. During the second Plan period, state revenue, it was said, would be about 30 percent of national income, and investments in "capital construction" were expected to approximate 40 percent of state expenditures. Population was expected to continue to increase by at least 2 percent per year.

Projecting these estimates and norms into the future, they suggest that in very rough terms the Chinese Communists estimated that by 1962, the final year of the second Plan period, Communist China would have a national income of close to $60 billion, a population of almost 700 million, and a per capita national income of approximately $90.

The Chinese Communists also stated toward the end of the first Plan period that during the second Plan, of total "capital construction" expenditures (averaging between $7 and 8 billion annually) they hoped to invest 60 percent in industry and 10 percent in agriculture, figures representing average annual investments during 1958-62 of about $3 billion to $4 billion per year in industry and about $700 million per year in agriculture. The minimum level of annual "capital accumulation" which they projected for the years 1958-62 was 20 percent of total national income, involving an average of about $11 billion per year over the five years. The initial production targets for the second Five Year Plan, announced in 1956, called for a 70 to 75 percent rise in the value of gross industrial and agricultural output, a 100 percent increase in the value of gross industrial production, and a 35 percent rise in the value of gross agricultural production. 10/

The future pattern as projected at the end of the first Plan period, therefore, involved a continuation of the process of industrialization and overall economic growth which was initiated during the years 1953-57. It appeared in 1957, however, that numerous basic problems were catching up with the regime, and that the pace of development might have to be slowed down. But then, in 1958, Peking launched its "great leap forward" and started dramatic new programs, involving the organization of the peasantry into communes and the development of small-scale industries which appeared to accelerate the pace of development (see Chapter Seven).

Annex to Chapter Two

THE USE OF CHINESE COMMUNIST STATISTICS

In view of the exaggerated and sometimes outright fantastic claims which the Chinese Communists have recently issued, some comment must be made on the credibility of Peking's statistics.

In examining Chinese Communist statistics, distinction should be made between three different periods. Up until late 1954, Peking's official statistics were generally stated in terms of percentage increases rather than as absolute figures. These percentages were often very misleading. Usually, the base figures were unclear, and for propaganda purposes every effort was made to exaggerate accomplishments. Then, from 1955 through 1957, the Chinese Communists published absolute figures which appeared to be fairly consistent and credible; and these statistics also included figures for earlier years.

More recently, however, beginning in early 1958, Peking has started to make claims which, although stated in absolute figures, challenge belief. Clearly, many of these most recent claims have been exaggerated, and some of them appear to be fantastic. Neither the basis of these claims nor Peking's motives in issuing them is yet clear, however; so it is necessary, at least until further information is available, to view them skeptically and treat them with caution.

This study is based principally upon the figures issued by Peking between 1954 and the end of 1957. 11/ These figures appeared to be designed as much for internal use as for external propaganda. It is clear that the Chinese Communists need usable statistical material for their own planning and control. As detailed studies of Soviet statistics have indicated, falsification of data poorly serves the Communists' own internal purposes. In data about particular plants, or industries, and in preliminary targets issued for general propaganda purposes, Peking clearly distorted and exaggerated some statistics even during the 1954-57 period, but overall year-end statistics appeared to be credible in general terms. In line with Soviet practices, the Chinese Communists often tended to leave unfavorable data unreported rather than falsifying them, but such gaps can be filled indirectly by careful students (see Hollister, op. cit., p. XIX ff.).

This does not mean that any and all Chinese Communist statistics issued even in the years prior to 1958 can be taken at face value, however. Peking itself admits that it has had numerous statistical difficulties. Statistical standards have only gradually been worked out, and statistical measures have undergone numerous adjustments. Some of these standards and measures in themselves exaggerate output figures. The comprehensiveness of statistical coverage has changed, and some increases in output may well be attributable to broader coverage. Also, the State Statistical Bureau has altered the price base for its calculations in different periods.

Peking's official statistics must be treated cautiously, therefore, but at least up through 1957 they are, on the whole, meaningful, and they have been used as the basis of this study. In time, as more Western statisticians study the individual segments of the Chinese economy, it will be possible to adjust these figures and arrive at more judicious estimates. The work of Hollister and Liu, already referred to, plus the research of Alexander Eckstein, Wu Yuan-li, Li Choh-Ming and others, is steadily contributing to this process. Li Choh-Ming's recent book, <u>Economic Development of Communist China</u>, University of California Press, Berkeley and Los Angeles, 1959, makes an important contribution to the problem of dealing with Chinese Communist statistics. Much work remains to be done, however.

Chapter Three

INDUSTRIALIZATION DURING THE FIRST PLAN PERIOD

The modern factory is the prime symbol of economic development and national power for the Chinese Communists, and the Peking regime has stated that its long-range goal is to "transform China from an agricultural into an industrial nation" in which 70 percent of the gross output will come from industry and 60 percent of industrial output from heavy industries. During the first Five Year Plan period, a majority of investment and construction work in China was concentrated upon the hundreds of new or expanded industrial plants included in the Plan, and despite numerous difficulties and bottlenecks, China's industrial capacity and production developed rapidly.

Actually, production increased at a more rapid rate than capacity, as the Chinese Communists made every effort to ensure maximum utilization of the industrial plant inherited from past regimes. Many of the largest new industrial projects started during 1953-57 required five to six years for completion, and their capacity could not affect industrial output figures until the second Plan period. During 1957, in fact, Peking made the statement that whereas it hoped that by the end of the second Five Year Plan 50 percent of industrial output would come from new and reconstructed enterprises completed after 1952, such enterprises accounted for only 15 percent of industrial output in 1957. This statement suggested, moreover, that during 1953-57 output from plants already existing in 1952 had doubled. But since these older plants were operating near capacity levels in 1957, an increase of only 5 percent in their output was projected for 1958-62.

The combination of new factories and the intensive use of old ones made possible the large production increases claimed by the Chinese Communists. Peking's official statistics indicate that during the first Plan period gross industrial production rose by 119 percent, and output of modern industry by 133 percent, capital goods production by 204 percent, and consumer goods output by 85 percent (see Appendix Table 1). In addition, the output of individual and cooperative handicraftsmen was said to have risen almost 70 percent during the five years. The development of the machine-building industry -- of central importance among the heavy industries -- increased output by about 300 percent by the end of the Plan period.

The course of this industrial development during the five year period was erratic, however, due in part to fluctuations in agricultural output. The Chinese Communists were fully aware of the fundamental dependence of the entire economy's growth on the agricultural sector, as summed up in the following statement in mid-1957 from Hsueh Hsi, one of the principal theoretical journals of the Peking regime:

The implementation of our first Five year Plan proves, that whenever a good crop harvest was gathered, light industry developed at a greater rate, the domestic market became active, export supplies grew ample, state revenue showed increases, the people's living standard rose to a higher level, and the relationship between national construction and the people's livelihood became harmonious, and whenever there was a crop failure the opposite was the case. The different rates of economic growth in the past five years were mainly attributable to harvest conditions. As ours is an agricultural country, the effect of agriculture on our national economy is most tremendous and extensive. It is calculated that about half the value of industrial production during the first Five Year Plan depends on raw materials supplied by agriculture and about 80 percent of the value of consumer goods depends on raw materials supplied by agriculture. In terms of value, about 80 percent of the commodities supplied on the domestic market consist of farm produce and processed farm products. Of the total value of export goods, farm produce and processed farm products account for 75 percent. About 20 to 24 percent of railway transportation and 40 to 50 percent of highway and waterway transportation are affected by agriculture. All of this has its effects on state revenue. During the first Five Year Plan, over 50 percent of the state revenue has come directly from agriculture and from industrial production, commerce, foreign trade, and communications and transport that are connected with agriculture. [Agriculture is also] the main source of capital for construction of heavy industry.

Thus, for instance, whereas gross industrial output was claimed to have increased by over 30 percent in both 1953 and 1956 -- following the good crops of the previous years -- the claimed increase in 1954 was under 20 percent, and in 1955 it was under 10 percent, due in large part to the poor agricultural crops in 1953 and 1954. Similarly, fluctuations in individual industrial sectors, in consumer goods, in the capital goods industry as a whole, and even in the machine-building industry can be related to the crop variations of the last years. In addition, poor planning also played a role in causing these fluctuations.

Accompanying the expansion of industrial plant and the growth of industrial output during the first Plan period, there also were basic changes in the geographical distribution of industry as well as in its institutional framework in China. The first Five Year Plan involved a conscious attempt to disperse industry by building up new centers in the interior, far from the traditional coastal concentrations of industry. This was clearly indicated by the fact that of the 694 so-called "above norm" industrial projects (see footnote 3, Ch. 2, p. 102) scheduled to be started during the first Plan, 427 -- or over two thirds -- were slated to be built in locations other than the coastal provinces. A great deal of construction was planned for Manchuria, since this constituted China's only existing base of heavy industry, but cities such as Shanghai were given relatively low priority in the Plan, and many of the new factories were located in remote northwest and southwest China -- areas which had previously been almost completely lacking in modern industry.

The most important institutional change in industry during the first Plan period took place in 1955-56, during what the Chinese Communists subsequently called "the great revolution in our social system" which, they claimed, solved in the main "the contradiction between individual economy and socialist industrialization and the contradiction between capitalist ownership and socialist ownership." At the start of the first Five Year Plan, the state had owned about 50 percent of modern industry in China accounting for roughly 60 percent of modern industrial output, and the so-called "general line" had prescribed a step-by-step socialization of industry through several intermediary stages of "state capitalism," with each stage increasing state control over remaining private enterprises. This process proceeded gradually until 1956.

Then, in one quick campaign, the Communists converted approximately 70,000 private industrial enterprises, including 90 percent of all industry not already under complete state ownership, into "joint state private enterprises," in effect practically eliminating private industrial enterprise in China. The significance of this move lay in the fact that not only did it complete socialization of industry in China much earlier than had originally been scheduled but it also, in effect, transformed the Chinese managerial class from private entrepreneurs into state employees who were forced to continue contributing their skills and experience to the task of industrialization under Communist control. This was apparently carried out with a minimum of disruption to production.

In the expansion of industrial capacity and output which took place in China under the first Five Year Plan, basic heavy industries such as iron and steel underwent the most rapid expansion. Raw materials, fuels, and electric power made impressive progress too, but the Chinese Communists admitted that lags in certain industries in these fields created serious bottlenecks which posed problems for continued development. The metallurgical and machine-building industries also made big strides, and important new industries producing items such as alloy steels, trucks, automatic lathes, and large electrical turbines were established in China for the first time. The development of consumer goods industries, however, lagged behind domestic demands and needs.

The iron and steel industry has received top priority in the Chinese Communists' program, and by concentrating first on restoring and expanding the Japanese-built steel mills at Anshan in Manchuria, the Peking regime achieved substantial results in expanding output during 1953-57. During the first years of the Five Year Plan, Anshan became the major industrial showcase in China, and it remains so today, for with Soviet assistance Anshan has been built up with the most modern type of new machinery. Construction plans for Anshan during 1953-60, covering the first Five Year Plan period and three years of the second Plan period, called for 48 major construction or reconstruction projects there. And a great deal of construction work was done under these plans during the first Plan period. The Chinese Communists also restored or expanded minor steel producing facilities at Taiyuan, Maanshan, Lungyen, Tientsin, and Shanghai. In addition, preliminary work was started at Paotow and Wuhan on two new steel centers of major size which may eventually be comparable to Anshan in importance.

On the eve of the first Five Year Plan, in 1952, steel production in China was reported to be 1.35 million tons, and in mid-1955 the Plan target was set at 4.12 million tons for 1957. This goal was surpassed. The 1957 production, according to official claims, totaled 5.35 million tons.

An initial second Plan target for 1962 was set at 10.5 to 12 million tons.

Development of iron mining and pig iron output accompanied the development of the steel industry. The Chinese Communists claim to have discovered large new deposits of iron ore. During 1957 they asserted that China has iron ore reserves totaling over 11 billion tons, of which 4.7 billion tons are said to be proven reserves--a claim which compares with prewar estimates ranging from under 1 billion to about 2 billion tons, and a UN 1954 estimate of about 4.2 billion tons. Then, in a broadcast of late December 1958, they asserted that new discoveries in 1958 had brought "known deposits" to 100 billion tons, placing Communist China second in iron ore reserves among the nations of the world. These claims must be viewed with skepticism, but undoubtedly important new resources have been discovered. And pig iron output has steadily risen. Output during the first Plan period increased, according to official claims, from 1.9 million tons in 1952 to 5.9 million tons in 1957.

There is every reason to take seriously both the Chinese Communist claims for the 1953-57 period and their future plans for increased iron and steel output, even if production figures and targets may be somewhat exaggerated. Although China's raw material base for a steel industry is not comparable to that existing in countries such as the United States and the USSR -- China, in view of its resources of both iron ore and coking coal, probably has the capacity to become the leading steel producer in Asia. In early 1958, the Chinese Communists proclaimed that they hoped to surpass Britain's steel output by 1972. More recently they have made fabulous claims about increased output during 1958, asserting that steel output reached 11 million tons, and they have set a production target of about 18 million tons for 1959.

At the same time, since the Chinese have selected British -- as well as Japanese -- production as points of reference in their own targets, the wide disparities evident in a per capita comparison must be noted. Crude steel output for 1958, for example, shows the following:

Country	Output per capita (lbs.)
Communist China	37
Japan	288
United Kingdom	853

Other heavy industries developed considerably during the first Plan period. Cement output rose from 2.9 million tons in 1952 to 6.7 million in 1957, exceeding the Plan target of 6.0 million; and then Peking announced a 1962 target of 12.5 to 14.5 million tons. In the field of chemicals, production of chemical fertilizer rose from 180,000 tons in 1952, to 755,000 in 1957.

The Chinese Communists placed great importance in their first Plan upon developing industries producing various types of machinery and equipment. For example, the Plan called for completing one automotive factory with an annual capacity of 30,000 trucks, starting a second which would ultimately turn out 60,000 a year, and beginning work on a tractor plant to have an annual production capacity of 15,000 tractors. The actual number of motor vehicles produced in 1957 was 10,000.

The plan also included many new plants to produce heavy machinery, power-generating equipment, machine tools, instruments, textile machinery, electric wire and cable, ships, and other items in the heavy industry category. During the Plan period, annual output of metal-cutting machine tools was raised, according to official claims, from slightly under 14,000 in 1952 to almost 23,000 in 1957. In 1952, electric motors with a capacity of 640,000 kw were manufactured; by 1957, output was more than doubled.

On an experimental basis, at least, China turned out such new products as 15,000 kw turbines and certain types of automatic lathes. By 1956, China was also able to build many types of mining and manufacturing machinery. It turned out in that year about 200 locomotives and 6,600 railway freight and passenger cars. It produced equipment for small-scale factories such as sugar mills, as well as sizable amounts of textile machinery. Altogether, the Chinese Communists claim that during 1953-56 they were able to manufacture 2.3 million cotton textile spindles and 60,000 looms.

Every year numerous new factories producing machinery were built in China. In 1957 alone, plans called for starting work on over 50 large machine-building factories for metallurgical and mining equipment, 20 power equipment plants, eight machine tool factories, and four locomotive plants. At year-end it was claimed that during 1957 work had been started or continued on 642 "above-norm" industrial and mining projects, of which 178 were completed during the year. The Chinese also started constructing facilities to produce jet aircraft -- probably intended to be, at the start, an assembly plant rather than a plant capable of producing all the many items required for aircraft output -- and with Soviet help, they began building a small atomic reactor. Both the aircraft plant and reactor were in operation by 1958.

The progress in developing modern transport, fuels, and power during the first Plan period was not inconsiderable, but as 1957 drew to a close the Chinese Communists admitted that the strain on transportation, fuels, and power to support their entire industrialization program was a major problem. Transportation development in Communist China during the first Plan period focused upon railways, although highway development was also accorded some attention. The Plan called for constructing slightly over 4,000 kilometers (one kilometer equals about five eighths of a mile) of new railway trunk lines and branches, in addition to restoring about 6,000 kilometers of rail lines, and building or repairing upward of 10,000 kilometers of highway. By late 1957, the Chinese Communists claimed that during the Plan period they actually had completed about 5,000 kilometers of new railway lines and had built or repaired about 12,000 kilometers of highways.

The importance of many of the new railways and roads, built in remote interior provinces, is strategic and political, as well as economic. Roads to Tibet were built. One new rail link with the USSR via Outer Mongolia was completed, while another via Sinkiang was started. Considerable progress was made on a whole new north-south rail network deep in China's interior. But even including these additions, Communist China's entire railway network at the end of 1957 probably totaled only about 29,000 kilometers, and its usable road system amounted to about 240,000 kilometers (mostly unsurfaced). On either a per capita or per mile basis, China at the end of its first Plan still had one of the least well-developed systems of modern transportation of any major nation, and the inadequacy of rail transport continued to be a fundamental problem. Because of this, Peking set an initial target of 8,000 to 9,000 kilometers of new lines in the second Plan period.

Of all power sources in China, coal is by far the most important, and coal is also an important potential export commodity. Coal, either directly in steam engines or indirectly through thermopower electric plants, produces most of the power for modern industry and transportation in China, as well as fuel for home consumption. China is well endowed with coal deposits and undoubtedly has the largest reserves in the Far East; good quality coking coal may be limited, however. Prewar estimates of these reserves varied, but a figure of roughly 250 billion tons was widely accepted. A UN survey in 1952 had placed total reserves at 444 billion tons. Now, however, the Chinese Communists claim that they have made new discoveries, greatly raising estimates of the nation's coal reserves to between 1 and 1.5 trillion tons, of which 44.2 billion are proven reserves. Whether or not these estimates are accurate, there is no doubt that at this stage in China's development, the problem is not a lack of reserves but the task of getting coal out of the ground in sufficient quantities.

The first Five Year Plan called for impressive coal development. Among other things, the Plan as of mid-1955 called for coal mining projects which were expected to result in 31 coal mines in China producing over a million tons annually each. In overall production terms, the Plan scheduled a rise in coal output from 64 million tons in 1952 to 113 million tons in 1957. In early 1958, Peking asserted that 1957 production had amounted to 128.62 million tons, surpassing the Plan target. It should be noted that many Western observers discount Chinese coal statistics because of a conviction that they are inflated -- perhaps by as much as 10 to 20 percent -- by the inclusion of weight of impurities which must be removed by washing before the coal can be used.

However, as coal output rose, domestic demand also increased, and during the years 1953-57 there were many indications that Communist China, despite claimed production increases, experienced real coal shortages. It was decided early in 1957 to reduce coal distribution to government and military organizations by up to 20 percent, to cut the number of holidays for coal miners, to reduce allocations to household consumers substantially, and to cut quotas for rural areas. As in the case of iron and steel, it was decided that, in the future, more attention would be paid to developing the output of small mining establishments which could be put into operation fairly quickly, rather than concentrating merely on big mine projects. All of these facts suggested that despite production increases in 1953-57, coal supplies were still lagging behind domestic needs at the end of the first Five Year Plan, and big increases in coal output were therefore scheduled for the second Plan period. At the end of the first Plan, an initial target for production in 1962 was tentatively set at 190-210 million tons.

Of the numerous power projects scheduled in China's first Five Year Plan, the most important ones called for construction of 15 large thermal plants each with a capacity of over 50,000 kw. Most of these were to be in Manchuria, Northwest China and Southwest China. Some hydroelectric projects were also included in the regime's plans, and the largest of these called for expansion of the capacity of the Japanese-built hydroelectric station at Fengmen in Manchuria. The total increase in the capacity of commissioned new plants, both thermal and hydroelectric, called for by the Plan was over 2 million kw.

By the end of the first Plan period, the Chinese Communists claimed that total power output had been raised from 7.26 billion kwh in 1952 to 19.03 billion kwh in 1957, surpassing the Plan target of 15.9 billion kwh. During this period, Peking started making grandiose plans for long-term development of its hydroelectric potential, including a detailed plan for harnessing the Yellow River, and in 1957 it claimed to have started preliminary work on five major hydroelectric plants which it said would ultimately have a capacity of 3.3 million kw. At the end of the first Plan it set an initial 1962 target for total power output at over 40 billion kwh.

Development of the petroleum industry in China was relatively slow during 1953-57, and this was the one crucial heavy industrial field in which the Chinese Communists admitted frankly their failure to achieve planned increases. The Five Year Plan called for raising annual petroleum output from 436,000 tons to slightly over 2 million tons, but actual output fell far short of this goal. Claimed production in 1957 amounted to only 1.46 million tons, of which natural oil constituted 800,000 tons, the remainder of the total coming from oil shale.

Extensive prospecting for new oil reserves went on during the first Plan period, and Peking has reported discoveries of important new deposits in the Tsaidam Basin, the Karamai region, and Szechuan; but it still appears as if China may be seriously lacking in petroleum, however, even though it is now claimed that reserves total 5.9 billion tons. Most of the increases in output achieved during 1953-57 were the result of expansion of the production started by the Nationalists at Yumen in Northwest China, and restoration of the shale oil industry started by the Japanese in Manchuria; and despite the great efforts Peking has made to increase output, there is every indication that China will experience a shortage of domestic petroleum supplies for a long time to come.

As stated earlier, although consumer goods industries did develop significantly during the first Plan period, they were given a relatively low priority in Peking's total program, and the output of consumer goods failed to keep up with growing demand, particularly in poor crop years. This fact is well illustrated by the textile industry, which is of basic importance in China. By 1957, the Chinese Communists claimed that with the completion of 10 plants scheduled to be finished before the end of the year, new construction during 1953-57 would total 40 large mills with 1.6 million spindles, bringing China's total capacity to over 7 million spindles capable of producing 5.6 million bales of cotton yarn a year. Starting with an output of 3.6 million bales of yarn in 1952, Peking set its output target for 1957 at 5 million bales. As new plants were developed, actual output did increase, but it fluctuated wildly from 4.1 million bales in 1953 to 5.2 million in 1956, and then dropped to 4.6 million in 1957, being influenced more by the availability of raw cotton than by plant capacity.

Output of cotton cloth followed a similar pattern, and in 1957 production amounted to only 150 million bolts, a big drop from the claimed output of 174 million in 1956, and short of the Plan target of 164 million for 1957.

Nationwide rationing of cotton cloth was introduced in 1954, and in 1957 the individual cloth ration was cut to a new low level. The principal reason for this stringent situation was the shortage of raw cotton. A good cotton crop in 1957 made possible a substantial increase in textile output during 1958, the first year of the second Plan period, but the year-to-year fluctuations in output of textiles--and some other important consumer goods--highlighted in very clear terms the direct dependence of much Chinese industry upon the performance of the agricultural sector of China's economy during the first Plan period. And this dependence of industrialization upon agriculture in China is not likely to change soon. In the future, as in the past, the peasantry will be a crucial factor in the Chinese Communists' plans.

Chapter Four

SOVIET ASSISTANCE FOR CHINA'S INDUSTRIALIZATION

During the first Five Year Plan period, Communist China's entire industrialization program was geared to and dependent upon Soviet promises to help build key industrial and related projects in China by providing large-scale technical assistance and by selling the Chinese essential equipment, mostly on a barter basis and only partly financed by Soviet loans. Soviet technicians and equipment were indispensable to the Peking regime during this period. It is remarkable, however, that Soviet financial assistance to Chinese economic development has been so small, in view of the fact that Communist China is the largest and most important of Moscow's allies. The Chinese Communists have had to pay their own way in relations with the Russians for the most part, exporting agricultural and other commodities to the Soviet bloc in exchange for the equipment and technical assistance received.

The framework for Sino-Soviet economic relations was first established in early 1950, when the Russians and Chinese signed several important economic agreements. Moscow granted China a five-year $300 million loan and promised to help in the construction or rehabilitation of 50 specific projects in China. The initial arrangements for barter trade between the two countries were also made at that time. Soon thereafter, Communist China entered the Korean conflict, and large-scale military aid flowed from the USSR to China -- exactly how much it was has never been revealed. Then, after the Korean fighting had reached a stalemate, and when the Chinese Communists were making initial preparations to start their first Five Year Plan, Peking sent a high-powered delegation to Moscow to negotiate for further economic assistance from the Russians.

Quite clearly, the whole scope and character of China's first Five Year Plan was dependent upon the kind of assistance which could be obtained from the Russians, and the negotiations which went on in Moscow from late 1952 until mid-1953 probably involved hard bargaining. Finally, it was announced in the fall of 1953, after the death of Stalin, and after the first year of China's Five Year Plan was almost finished, that the Soviet Union had agreed to help build 91 more specific large-scale construction projects in China. These "141 key Soviet aid projects" 1/ became the foundation of China's Five Year Plan. Roughly a year later, in late 1954, Khrushchev and Bulganin made the first official visit of any top-level Soviet leaders to China, and while there, they raised the number of "Soviet aid projects" to 156, announced a second Soviet loan to China equivalent to $130 million, and committed the USSR to provide the Chinese with $100 million of equipment and supplies in addition to earlier commitments. Then, in early 1956, Mikoyan raised the number of "Soviet aid projects" to 211 by committing the USSR to assist China in constructing 55 more major projects requiring an additional $625 million worth of Soviet equipment and supplies.

The 211 major Soviet aid projects -- of which over 140 were scheduled to be started and close to 60 finished before the end of 1957 -- were the core of China's first Five Year Plan. Most projects were in the field of heavy industry, including steel and other metallurgical factories; machine tool and engineering plants; iron, coal, and nonferrous metal mines; automotive, tractor, and aeronautical factories; chemical, synthetic, and plastics plants; factories for electrical and radio equipment; petroleum installations and refineries; railway and other transportation projects; and scientific research institutes. The Soviet Union has provided the technical assistance necessary for these projects and has sold to China the equipment required for the projects.

As Peking's second Five Year Plan got underway, Moscow made further pledges to help build major construction projects in China. In the fall of 1958, a Sino-Soviet agreement was signed in Moscow committing the Russians to give technical assistance to the Chinese on 47 more projects. Then, in early 1959, the Russians made promises to help build an additional 78 projects. At the same time, they committed themselves to sell to the Chinese during the nine year 1959-1967 period, $1.25 billion worth of equipment for these projects. It should be noted that, contrary to the interpretation placed on this commitment by some writers, there is no evidence that a Soviet credit is involved. Moreover, only part of the equipment required for these latest projects is to be provided by the Russians, for the Chinese will supply much of it themselves.

Just how important Soviet technical assistance has been was revealed by Chairman of the State Planning Commission Li Fu-Chun in mid-1955. "On the 156 [the total at the time] industrial projects which the Soviet Union is helping us to build," he stated, "she assists us through the whole process from start to finish, from geological surveying, selecting construction sites, collecting basic data for designing, designing, directing the work of construction, installation, and getting into production, and supplying technical information on new types of products, right down to directing the work of the manufacture of new products." In early 1958, Peking stated that about 7,000 Soviet experts had worked in China up to that time, but some responsible sources have estimated that there may have been as many as 10,000 to 20,000 (and if military experts were included the figure would probably be higher). Since 1957 there have been reports that the number of Soviet experts in China has been reduced, but how far this has gone is not yet clear.

The Russians have not only sent industrial experts to work on major projects in China, they have also given the Chinese technical assistance of various other sorts as well. Soviet advisers have played a significant role in the institutional reorganization -- following the Soviet pattern -- of industries, planning organizations, budgetary methods, tax systems, labor organizations, wage systems, and the industrial management structure in China. They have advised the Chinese in the reorganization of their educational system on the Soviet model so that it now concentrates upon the task of turning out technicians to work for the state. The Chinese claim that this reorganization enabled them to increase the total number of Chinese technicians, broadly defined, from 170,000 in 1952 to 800,000 at the end of 1957.

Through the Sino-Soviet Scientific and Technical Cooperation Commission, established in 1954, the Chinese had received from the Russians by mid-1957,

600 kinds of blueprints for factories, shops, and enterprises, 1,700 working drawings for the production and installation of machines, and other important technical data. Reportedly, 90 percent of the new products manufactured by Communist China's machine-building industry during 1953-57 was based on designs provided by the USSR. Over 7,000 Chinese university and graduate students went to the Soviet bloc -- mostly to the Soviet Union and the majority for technical training -- in the seven years up to June 1957. And many Chinese workers went for short-term in-service training in Soviet enterprises during this same period. In late 1957, Peking stated that close to 7,000 workers, technicians, and factory administrators had received training in the USSR during the first Plan period. All of these forms of Soviet technical aid helped fill the serious gaps in China's own supply of technical skills.

In addition to providing technical assistance, the Soviet Union has made definite assurances, as stated earlier, that it would make available for sale to the Chinese Communists essential equipment and supplies required for many large-scale projects in China. In early 1956, Khrushchev stated that the USSR up to that time had committed itself to supply $1.4 billion worth of equipment and supplies for 156 key projects in China, and Mikoyan's commitment in 1956 to supply $625 million more raised the total to over $2 billion for the 211 "Soviet aid projects" decided upon during the Chinese Communists' first Plan period. The recent commitment to supply $1.25 billion worth of equipment and supplies during 1959-67 seems to involve a promise of roughly $140 million annually in the years immediately ahead.

The economic requirements of supplying certain of Peking's industrial needs have certainly become a factor which Moscow must consider in its overall economic planning; but, although Soviet commitments have imposed a burden upon Russian productive capacity, this burden may not have been excessively large in terms of the total capacities of the Soviet economy. There have been some indications, however, that exports of machinery and equipment in barter arrangements with Communist China have constituted a significant drain on certain of the satellites in Eastern Europe. 2/

All in all, the Russians seem to have been unwilling, however, to assist the Chinese very substantially in carrying the financial burden of China's industrial development program. The Soviet Union has not given Communist China a single free economic grant as far as is known, and even the volume of Soviet loans and credits to the Chinese has been small in terms of China's economic situation and needs.

As mentioned previously, the only two long-term Soviet economic loans to Communist China which have been publicly announced were the 1950 and 1954 loans totaling $430 million. Since 1954, the Chinese Communists have been repaying the first $300 million loan (and the 1 percent interest charges) in installments which will continue over ten years through 1963. No detailed data have ever been revealed about utilization of the second loan. Communist China's published budgets indicate that all foreign credits had been utilized by 1957. In 1958 Peking did not receive any further foreign credits, and apparently it does not expect any in 1959. The two above-mentioned loans probably total less than half the value of Soviet removals and destruction of equipment in Manchuria in 1945.

Although the 1950 and 1954 loans are the only specific ones which have ever been announced, the Chinese Communists in mid-1957 stated that over the eight year 1949-57 period they had received loans and credits of all kinds from the Soviet Union totaling approximately $2.24 billion, and they asserted that about $1.31 billion of this had been received during the first Five Year Plan, 1953-57 period. The fact that all but $430 million of this has never been publicly accounted for suggests that most of the rest of the overall figure of $2.24 billion consisted of military assistance and financial transactions other than current economic aid. It is likely that much of it represented charges against the Chinese for Russian military equipment and services, and for the transfer of Soviet shares in Sino-Soviet joint stock companies which were turned over to exclusive Chinese ownership in 1954-55.

By the end of the first Five Year Plan period, Communist China had clearly reached the bottom of the barrel of past Soviet loans and credits. Chinese receipts from Soviet aid can be estimated for years prior to 1956 (see Appendix Table 7), and, starting in 1956, Peking began publishing in its budgets specific figures on receipts from foreign loans each year. These budget figures reveal that Communist China received only $50 million in foreign aid in 1956, $10 million in 1957, and none in 1958. By contrast, it is estimated that Chinese repayment to the Soviet Union and servicing of past Soviet loans and credits totaled $260 million in 1956, and $271 million in 1957.

Peking encountered increasingly serious balance of payments problems from 1956 on, and the Russians made a minor concession by agreeing to let the Chinese postpone some of their scheduled 1957 exports to the Soviet Union until 1958. But as Soviet credits declined, and Chinese repayments to the Soviet Union increased, Peking was forced to export ever increasing amounts of goods to the USSR, and China's export surplus in Sino-Soviet trade steadily grew during 1956-58 (see Chapter Eight). It was expected by many observers that Mao Tse-tung would discuss economic aid on his visit to the Soviet Union in the fall of 1957, but no additional Soviet loans or credits were announced either then or during 1958.

Unless further financial assistance is forthcoming in the future, Peking faces increasingly difficult problems in financing its industrial development during the second Plan period, and the burdens imposed on China's agriculture and foreign trade, which are already very heavy, will become increasingly onerous. It is very possible that the lack of external financial aid, and the increasing difficulty of paying for capital goods imports from the USSR, were significant factors influencing Peking to rely more on its own resources and to embark upon its radical domestic programs to establish communes and decentralized small-scale industries in 1958.

Chapter Five

AGRICULTURE AND THE PEASANT

Although the Chinese Communists' primary economic aim is industrialization, agriculture remains the foundation of the Chinese economy.
It was in the field of agriculture that Peking encountered the most serious
problems during its first Five Year Plan, and some of the thorniest questions for the future focus upon agriculture. It is the agricultural sector
of the economy which must provide food for a growing urban and industrial population, the bulk of export products to pay for imports of essential
capital goods, and increased raw materials for industry.

The Chinese Communists' basic approach to agriculture during the
first Plan period focused upon institutional reorganization of farming to
give the state maximum control over the peasants and the land. The most
dramatic development affecting agriculture during the first Plan period
was collectivization of the land. The land distribution program, which was
an important feature of the Chinese Communists' struggle for power, was
largely completed by 1952. Even before it was completed Peking had
initiated a "gradual," step-by-step program involving organization of
peasants first into mutual aid teams, then into agricultural producers'
cooperatives, and finally into full collectives. The "general line" of the
regime formalized this program, and at the start of the first Plan period
the Chinese Communists said they hoped to have one fifth of the peasants in cooperatives by 1957.

However, the poor crop years at the start of the Plan led the regime
to take increasingly drastic steps to achieve control over the peasants
and their output. In the fall of 1953, a state monopoly of grain and nationwide rationing were instituted. Finally, in mid-1955, Mao Tse-tung decided
to speed up collectivization in a dramatic fashion. A tremendous organiz-
ing drive took place, and during a period of about one year over 96 percent
of China's peasants were brought under the control of roughly a million
agricultural producers' cooperatives, and 88 percent of these were then
converted into "higher stage cooperatives" (collectives). By the end of
1956, Chinese agriculture was, for all practical purposes, collectivized,
and less than 5 percent of agricultural land in China remained under individual private proprietorship. During 1957, in the process of consolidating collectivization, the number of producer cooperatives dropped to about
three quarters of a million.

This phenomenal collectivization drive was undoubtedly one of the
greatest gambles in "social engineering" in history; it was followed by
an even more radical reorganization of agriculture which placed the
peasants in communes during 1958 (see Chapter Seven). These events
provide eloquent testimony to the political power of the Peking regime.
The Chinese Communists encountered less effective peasant resistance
than the Russians had met during their collectivization drive. Only minor
forms of resistance took place (there were some reports of killing of
cattle and pigs, and the cutting down of trees). But collectivization was

clearly imposed on China's peasants against their will, despite the fact that the Communists accomplished it by methods which might be called "coercive persuasion" and maintained that the whole process was voluntary. In the years preceding 1955, the Peking regime had undermined the possibility of effective peasant opposition by destroying the power and influence of the landlords and rich peasants (several million of whom were liquidated); by establishing strong political control at the village level; and by achieving dominance over the peasants' markets, sources of supplies, and credit.

Collectivization did not automatically solve Peking's problems, however. Even with this degree of control the Chinese Communists could not know how the peasants would react over a period of years, and it is by no means clear whether in the long run the effects of collectivization on peasants' incentives and attitudes will have an adverse or favorable impact upon agricultural production. During collectivization, however, there was little evidence of overt resistance -- active or passive -- and the Chinese Communists encountered remarkably little effective sabotage by peasants.

Although by the end of the first Plan period the peasants had been effectively organized, there were many signs that the collectives were not yet working very efficiently, and 1957 proved to be a difficult year in the countryside. Many collectives were in a confused state. Some of them withheld grain and other products from the state. The process of "consolidating" the collectives -- that is, making them work -- proceeded, however, and Peking made every effort to develop them into functioning organizations under state control. Large numbers of political workers, government employees, and students were sent into the countryside on assignments to work in the collectives. And Peking's leaders were forced to devote increasing attention to agricultural problems.

Apart from reorganizing the institutional basis for farming in China, the Chinese Communists accomplished a good deal in the field of water conservation during the first Plan period, and literally millions of peasants were organized to work on irrigation and flood control projects. Some of these projects, such as the Hwai River project, the Chinkiang reservoir on the upper Yangtze River, and the Kwanting reservoir on the Yungting River, were on a very large scale. Plans were drawn up for a grandiose TVA-type of scheme in the Yellow River Valley, and some investigation was carried out in preparation for a similar scheme encompassing the entire Yangtze Valley. But the majority of the water conservation projects during the first Five Year Plan period were much smaller.

A considerable amount of land was reclaimed. The minimum target for reclamation during the first Plan period had been set at 6.5 million acres, and this was reportedly overfulfilled. During the first three years of the Plan period, according to official claims, roughly 6 million acres of wasteland were reclaimed, and then in 1956 alone reclaimed wasteland allegedly amounted to almost 5 million acres.

The Chinese Communists have made highly optimistic estimates of the amount of wasteland in China capable of being cultivated. One statement from Peking asserted that cultivable wasteland amounts to almost 250 million acres, that over 140 million acres of this have been surveyed, and that over 80 million acres have been found to be readily reclaimable.

However, these claims are dubious. Most unused land of this sort undoubtedly is marginal and would be very costly to reclaim. Although pre-Communist estimates of reclaimable land varied, qualified observers felt prior to 1949 that probably not more than 30 to 40 million acres of uncultivated land could be opened up without prohibitively high investment costs.

Actually, despite their claims concerning reclamation, the Chinese Communists in practice appear to have operated on the belief that increases in agricultural production must be obtained primarily from increases in the yields of land already cultivated. One of their main aims has been to increase the irrigated area on existing farmland, and they made significant progress on this both before and during the first Plan period. According to official Peking claims, Mainland China's irrigated area increased by over 13 million acres in 1950-52, by over 9 million acres during the initial three years of the first Plan, 1953-55, and subsequently, as a result of a big drive in the winter of 1955-56, it reportedly increased by almost 20 million acres in 1956 alone. Then, in late 1957, the Chinese Communists initiated a massive, nationwide program to develop irrigation, and Peking claimed that during 1957-58 over a hundred million peasants were organized to work on conservation projects, as a result of which the irrigated area in China was almost doubled. It is difficult to accept these specific claims, but there is little doubt that the irrigated area in China has been greatly expanded.

In addition to increasing crop acreage -- as distinct from cultivated land -- by irrigation and multiple cropping, the Chinese Communists also began during the first Plan period to put increased emphasis upon close planting of crops to improve land utilization and increase per acre output.

None of these efforts, however, could harness the weather, and China continued to be plagued by natural disasters. Floods were serious in 1953, and in 1954 the worst floods in many years affected about 27 million acres, or roughly one tenth of all cultivated land in the country. Disasters in 1956 were even worse -- 38.5 million acres were affected. And although 1957 was not as bad, it was still a year of adverse weather conditions. Despite all the Communists' work on conservation projects during the first Plan period, therefore, floods and droughts still constituted a basic problem in 1957, as they had in 1952.

Apart from conservation and reclamation work, the Chinese Communists also attempted during the first Five Year Plan period to combat pests with simple methods, introduce some improved seeds and tools, establish a new state-controlled farm credit system to replace the one disrupted by land reform, and assist agricultural production in various other ways. Millions of peasants were organized in anti-pest campaigns, and two to three million insecticide sprayers were sold. Mechanical innovations were confined for the most part to improved plows, close to three million of which were distributed -- in many areas, however, peasants claimed the plows were unusable.

Agricultural credit provided by the state increased slowly during 1953-55, and then rapidly in 1956, rising to about $1.4 billion in the latter year. Also, the Peking regime claimed by 1957 to have established roughly 15,000 so-called "agro-technical stations," 2,000 experimental seed farms,

35 agricultural schools, and over 200 "centers for agricultural research." Although in earlier years it seemed as if the Chinese Communists hoped to mechanize in the Soviet fashion, by the end of the first Plan period it was clear that this aim had been postponed. In 1957, only a few experimental areas and state farms were using tractors. Collectivization in China, in great contrast to collectivization in the Soviet Union, has been primarily an organizational rather than a technical revolution. But, by 1957, Peking had begun putting increased emphasis upon the need to develop modest, small-scale mechanization, a trend which could be significant in the future.

The Chinese Communists were very reluctant at the start of the first Plan period to invest a great deal in spreading the use of chemical fertilizers on a large scale -- a step which, as the experience of countries such as Japan indicates, can have a significant effect on per acre crop output. Circumstances gradually forced Peking to change its attitude on this problem, however, and the priority given both to imports and to home production of chemical fertilizer steadily rose. Chemical fertilizer output within China rose to 755,000 tons in 1957, and Peking then set an initial target of 6 million tons of domestic output in 1962, or almost eight times the amount produced in 1957.

Simply stated, however, the basic agricultural problems in China were so great that Peking's planned investments in agriculture during 1953-57 (for both agriculture and water conservation budgeted investments were under $300 million annually in 1953-55, and between $400 million and $500 million annually in 1956-57), were inadequate to meet the needs of the agricultural sector of the economy. Peking's primary emphasis in the field of agricultural investment was placed upon nonbudget investments -- by agricultural cooperatives, for example -- and it was claimed that during the years 1953-57 such investment was four to five times as large as agricultural capital construction included in the government budgets.

As the Plan period progressed, however, the pressure of agricultural problems forced Peking to invest more in agriculture than it had originally planned, and by the end of the first Plan, the Chinese Communists had devoted 10 percent of their total investments to agriculture, instead of the 7.6 percent they had originally planned. But even this increase in investments was insufficient to ensure fulfillment of Peking's optimistic initial targets for increased crop output during 1953-57.

At the start of the Five Year Plan, the Chinese Communists, perhaps misled by relatively good crop years in 1951 and 1952, asserted that grain output would be raised from almost 164 million tons in 1952 to roughly 213 million tons in 1957, a five year increase of 30 percent, amounting to about 50 million tons. 1/ But, in 1953 and 1954, very little progress was made towards this target, and the pessimistic outlook led the Chinese Communists in mid-1955 to reduce the Five Year Plan's 1957 target to 192.8 million tons, involving only a 17.6 percent increase over 1952.

After the good weather and crops in 1955, optimism soared again, and the regime announced a comprehensive 12 year agricultural plan calling for huge increases in per acre yields of grain ranging from 100 to 167 percent in different parts of the country. Then came the natural disasters of 1956, followed by poor weather again in 1957. The 1957 grain production was claimed to be 185 million tons. This figure, which did not include soya beans, represented an increase of perhaps 20 percent over the 1952 level, if soya beans are subtracted from the earlier statistics -- soya bean output in 1957 was almost 10 million tons, making a total of 195 million tons of grain and soya beans during the year. In 1958 Peking made fantastic production claims (see Chapter Seven). However, Communist China's grain output figures are particularly difficult to evaluate. A part of the claimed increase in production during the first Plan period may merely have represented improved and more complete crop reporting rather than actual increases in output.

A shortage of grain, in any case, certainly created fundamental stresses in the Peking regime's entire development program during its first Plan period, and grain was rationed to everyone in China from 1953 onward. One austerity campaign followed another, and during 1957 the grain ration was reduced from its already low level. Undoubtedly, starvation was kept to a minimum, due to the effectiveness of the state's distributive mechanism in providing at least minimum subsistence requirements to almost the whole population, but consumption levels were kept low. Moreover, despite the claims of record crops, reports of food shortages continued.

Peking hoped to replenish its depleted grain stocks during 1957 in order to provide a sound basis for starting the second Five Year Plan, but as of late 1957 there was much evidence of increasing official concern about shortcomings in agricultural production. Revision in the 12 year agricultural plan took place in 1957, and apparently the regime's goals were considerably modified. And at the end of the first Plan period, the preliminary second Plan target for grain output -- calling for production of 250 million tons in 1962 -- looked rather remote. In 1958 Peking claimed an increase of grain output to 375 million tons (see Chapter Seven).

The development of cotton production, the most important industrial crop in China, was extremely erratic during the first Plan period. More often than not during the five years, cotton output fell short of the yearly targets which had been established, and fluctuations in cotton production had a great impact on the economy as a whole. Claimed output in 1952 was 1.3 million tons, and the first Plan target was set at over 1.6 million tons. Actual output, however, dropped as low as 1.06 million tons in 1954, and then stabilized at around 1.5 million tons in 1955 and 1956. Cotton had a good year in 1957, with output reaching 1.64 million tons, according to official claims, and this was an important factor helping to set the stage for accelerated economic progress in 1958. But during most of the first Plan period, the supply fell far short of China's needs, resulting in nation-wide rationing of cotton and cotton cloth from 1954 onward, and leading to the severe cuts in the ration in 1957. Sizable imports of raw cotton from abroad were necessary in poor crop years to provide raw material for China's textile industry, and Chinese textile plants operated at below capacity even with the imports.

The whole problem of allocating land to either food crops or industrial crops has been a difficult one for the Chinese Communists, because they have been short of both food and agricultural raw materials. During the first Five Year Plan there was some shift from food crops to industrial crops, but by 1957 the grain shortage was such that the Chinese Communists declared there should be no more enlargement of acreage devoted to industrial crops for some time to come. They stated, for example, that acreage for cotton, sugar, and oil bearing crops should be maintained at about the 1957 level. Nonetheless, the second Five Year Plan, when first announced in late 1957, called for raising cotton output to 2.4 million tons by 1962, and the Communists asserted that although they planned to open up 2.5 million acres of virgin land in Northwest China for cotton cultivation during "the next few years," immediate increases in cotton output would have to be achieved by raising per acre yields on the 15 million acres or so devoted to cotton as of 1957.

The shortage of agricultural products in China during 1953-57 extended to other items besides grain and cotton. This was the result partly of the failure of output to reach planned targets and partly of the regime's determination to export whatever was necessary to pay for critically-needed industrial imports. Chinese consumers were particularly hard-hit by the scarcity of vegetable oils and pork, both of which are basic to the Chinese diet. Throughout the first Five Year Plan period there was a serious shortage of vegetable oils, for reasons similar to those causing the difficulties with cotton.

There was also a pork shortage. The peasants' reaction to government controls, and difficulties in formulating sound price policies, as well as a shortage of hog feed, were major causes of this shortage. Even according to official Chinese statistics, China's hog population dropped from 90 million in 1952 to 84 million in mid-1956. The Plan target was 138 million, and this had not even been approached by 1956. At the end of the Plan period, Peking claimed that the hog population had risen to over 125 million during 1957, but this was questionable, particularly in view of the fact that the regime formally introduced pork rationing during 1957.

Because of the many problems posed by agriculture, Peking's leaders during the last years of the first Plan period, began to put considerably increased emphasis upon the need to increase investment in, and attention to, agriculture. This was a very significant development. The decision to speed up collectivization in 1955-56 was probably motivated in part by a desire to organize agriculture into larger units in which investment could be better directed and controlled, and certainly from 1956 onward the state began to assume a greater responsibility for agricultural development. As mentioned earlier, in 1956 and again in 1958 the Chinese Communists forced great changes in cropping practices aiming particularly at double-cropping, close planting, and growing more intensive crops; they increased imports of chemical fertilizers and stepped up domestic production plans; and they initiated tremendous drives to build small-scale irrigation projects.

By the end of 1957 Peking claimed that overall agricultural output had increased in value by an average annual rate of 4.5 percent during the previous five years, but this almost certainly was an overestimate. At the end of the First Plan period, it still appeared that agriculture would continue to lag, to create basic pressures and strains, and to be the most critical sector of the economy for a long time to come. It looked, in fact, as if lags in the agricultural sector might well slow down the pace of Communist China's entire development program.

Chapter Six

SOME PROBLEMS FOR THE FUTURE

The lag in agricultural output was perhaps the most pressing domestic economic problem facing the Chinese Communist regime at the end of the first Five Year Plan, but there were other formidable problems as the regime turned to its goals for the second Five Year Plan, 1958-62. One of the most important in relation to China's long-range economic prospects was, and is, the staggering population problem. As stated earlier, the Chinese Communists now believe that their population is increasing at a rate of over 2 percent per year. This estimate appears to be based largely upon investigations during 1953, in scattered areas of China, which indicated a birth rate of 37 per thousand and a death rate of only 17 per thousand.

These figures may not be entirely accurate, but it is probable that China's population is indeed increasing at a rapid rate. Such factors as the development of hygiene and simple health facilities under Communist rule have undoubtedly reduced death rates, while in all probability birth rates remain high. As in many areas of the world, the industrial revolution in China is competing with the "Malthusian counterrevolution."

When the Communists first came to power in 1949, they refused to recognize that China faced a major population problem. Ideologically, they were violently opposed to Western population theories, and they scornfully dismissed the opinions of population experts as subversive "neo-Malthusianism." After the 1953 census, however, their attitudes on this issue underwent a fundamental change, and Peking's leaders, seemingly aware for the first time that rapid population growth creates disturbing problems, completely reversed their earlier position and started advocating various types of birth control measures. In time, birth control clinics were established widely, and propaganda on the subject was disseminated throughout the country. Although by the end of the first Plan period there was little evidence that significant results had been achieved, it looked at least as if Peking was developing machinery and methods which might be used to launch a major campaign attacking the problem, and there seemed little doubt that if they launched such a campaign, their political power and propaganda skill might enable them to achieve at least some results.

In 1958 -- the year of Peking's "great leap forward" -- the Chinese Communists seemed to revert to earlier attitudes. Although they did not formally renounce birth control, and birth control clinics continued operating, they publicly denounced one of China's strongest exponents of slowing population growth, began once again to extol the virtues of having a large population, and started emphasizing their labor shortage rather than overpopulation -- all of which seemed to downgrade the need for population control. Even with effective birth control, Communist China undoubtedly would undergo a major "demographic explosion." If present population growth rates continue, Mainland China may have a population of one billion in the 1980s.

Another basic economic problem in Communist China which was particularly serious during the first Plan period, and which will continue as long as Peking follows its present overall policies, is the economic burden of the regime's large military expenditures. The Communists have been trying simultaneously to build China into a military power of international standing and to develop it into a major industrialized nation. In one sense, these two aims have been complementary in China -- or at least they have not been so contradictory as they would have been if Peking's economic objectives had been defined less in power terms and more in welfare terms -- because the Chinese Communists' industrial development policy with its accent on heavy industry is designed to support military power.

Nonetheless, the purely military costs of fighting in, or supporting, foreign wars, and of maintaining and modernizing large military forces, have put a tremendous burden on the Chinese economy. Even after the 1953 truce in Korea, Peking's published budgetary expenditures for "national defense" continued to run between $2 billion and $3 billion a year, and they totaled over $12 billion during the first Five Year Plan period. Undoubtedly, there are, in addition, some military expenditures concealed in other items of the budget, so that actual military expenditures have probably been higher than these figures indicate. The Chinese Communists' annual expenditures on their military establishment alone have been several times as large as the total national budgets of Chinese governments before the Sino-Japanese War, and, as a consequence, the burden which the Chinese people and economy have had to carry has not been simply the costs of economic development -- it has consisted of the combined costs of ambitious militarization and industrialization.

During the last two years of the first Five Year Plan period, the strains on the Chinese economy forced the Communists to reduce expenditures in the "national defense" category somewhat, from $2.7 billion in 1955 to $2.6 billion in 1956, and to $2.3 billion in 1957. The budget for the first year of the second Plan period called for a further reduction to $2.1 billion. But there is still every indication that Peking intends to maintain a large and expensive military establishment which will continue to impose a heavy drain on China's limited resources. However, military personnel in Communist China is used as labor in many economic projects, both agricultural and industrial, and this reduces somewhat the real economic burden of maintaining large armed forces.

In its budget operations, Peking was able, during the first Plan period, to achieve a surplus of current revenues over current expenditures in every year except 1956. A paper "deficit" occurred in 1955, but this apparently was due to the appropriation that year of over $1 billion for bank "reserves" -- a bookkeeping transaction to reduce the carryover from recent years. In 1956, however, as the Chinese Communists tried to accelerate development rapidly, they did run into budgetary pressures. Urban wages and the labor force expanded beyond expectation, and the newly-formed collectives required more loans than originally planned for, while fiscal expenditures were tied up in large-scale construction projects which Peking was reluctant to curtail. Revenues lagged, and although the government tried to maintain stability by reducing its inventories, there was nonetheless a substantial increase in note issue.

As a result, the budget showed a deficit of roughly $775 million for 1956, and the Chinese Communists admitted that during the year they were forced to increase their note issue and to use up a sizable percentage of their reserves and stocks. This made it urgently necessary for them to try to replenish these reserves and stocks during 1957. The situation led Peking not only to cut down major investment plans for 1957, but also to plan a reduction in the overall budget from $12.9 billion in 1956 to $12.4 billion in 1957 -- the first general cutback in the total budget since the start of the Five Year Plan. As a result of the steps taken during this period of consolidation, the regime was able to build up its reserves and inventories during 1957, and the budget for 1958, when first announced, called for an increase in state income and expenditures by almost $1 billion.

It is remarkable that despite the heavy burden on the Chinese economy as a whole, the Peking regime, by and large, was very successful in combating price inflation during its first Five Year Plan. The dangers of inflation have been fully understood by Chinese Communist leaders, who knew well that runaway inflation in the late 1940s had been a major cause of the political, as well as the economic, disintegration of the Nationalist regime; and, for this reason, control of inflation was one of the first tasks which the Communists concentrated upon when they came to power. By 1952, despite a temporary setback during the Korean War, they had achieved price stability for all practical purposes, and during the early years of the Five Year Plan, this stability was well maintained through strict controls. Peking levied heavy taxes; it sopped up idle purchasing power through bond issues as well as through other savings campaigns; it established complete control of banking and the financial system; and it instituted nationwide rationing of essential commodities such as grain and cotton cloth.

By late 1956, however, the pressure of commodity shortages once again resulted in a certain amount of inflation, and the threat became more serious than at any time since the years immediately after 1949. The regime itself was forced to raise the prices of some commodities distributed through the state trading apparatus, and prices fluctuated disturbingly on the small free markets that were then still tolerated for nonrationed agricultural products. The price rises of late 1956 and 1957 were indicative of the fundamental strains on the Chinese economy, and in addition there was considerable repressed inflation in the form of commodity shortages which also caused concern to Communist Chinese leaders. But because of their high degree of control over the Chinese economy, the Communists were able to ease this situation by the start of their second Five Year Plan.

Unemployment was another problem which created difficulties for the Chinese Communists during their first Plan period, even though this may seem paradoxical in view of the fairly rapid development of industrial production which took place. Population increases and economic dislocations created more needs for new jobs than could be met during 1953-57. As stated earlier, official population figures indicate a staggering total population rise of roughly 65 million between 1952 and 1957. During this period, it is estimated, the farming population rose from 482 to 530 million, and total rural population jumped from 503 to 548 million, while the nonfarm population increased from 93 to 110 million, and total urban population from 72 to 92 million. Roughly 40 percent of the increase in urban areas -- or 8 million people -- was attributable to migration from rural areas rather than to the natural increase in urban areas.

Peking claimed that jobs in government and state-controlled enterprises (excluding the military) rose from about 10 million in 1952 to roughly 24 million in 1957; but since this included nationalized private enterprises, the real net increase in staff and workers was probably only between five and six million. In 1957, the number of staff and workers was actually reduced to a level lower than in 1956. Preliminary targets for the second Plan period indicated that the number of jobs for workers and employees in various branches of the national economy other than agriculture was slated to increase by six to seven million before the end of 1962, but this target did not appear to be very high in view of China's annual rate of population increase, which already amounts to 12 or 13 million people per year.

What Peking has labeled a "blind flow of peasants to the cities" -- resulting largely from difficult conditions in the countryside -- was a major cause of the Chinese Communists' urban unemployment problem, intensifying the problem already created by natural population increases. The regime tried to cope with this in several ways. It energetically attempted to repatriate peasants to the countryside, for one thing, and it also organized urban workers into labor gangs to work on various public works projects, along with the large numbers of workers in penal groups of forced laborers. In addition, many government employees and students were sent out of the cities. But the problem appeared to be far from solution at the end of the first Plan period. It may well have been one of the major reasons for the regime's increased efforts to utilize organized labor for economic development in irrigation and reclamation. It may also help to explain the decision in 1958 to institute semimilitary control over the rural population through the new comprehensive system of rural communes.

Although unemployment of unskilled labor presented Peking with one type of problem during its first Five Year Plan, Communist China's shortage of skilled laborers and technicians created difficulties of another sort. There is no doubt that shortages of skills have affected the industrialization program at every level. The Chinese Communist response to this problem has been energetic, however. For top-level technical skills, Peking relied heavily on Soviet experts during the first Plan period, but at the same time the Chinese Communists devoted tremendous efforts to training Chinese technicians and skilled workers at all levels.

This training program involved many things, including large-scale in-service training of workers, but the most notable development was the great expansion and complete reorganization of higher education in China. During the first Five Year Plan, enrollment in institutions of higher education more than doubled, rising to approximately 440,000 in 1957; and, in addition, the whole system of higher education in China was radically altered to emphasize technical training, and was based upon Soviet ideas of poly-technical education. Initial plans announced for the 1958-62 period set a target of 850,000 enrolled in institutions of higher learning by the end of the second Five Year Plan.

The dimensions of the overall problem of preparing the population of a country such as China for modernization and industrialization are illustrated by the literacy problem. The Chinese Communists have been active in the field of literacy training for adults ever since they came to power. In 1957 they claimed, in fact, to have taught 22 million illiterates how to read and write between 1949 and 1956. But in 1957, Communist China's Premier also admitted that over 70 percent of the total population was still illiterate. In comparison, the rate of illiteracy in India is estimated at about 82 percent.

Scientific development and training received high priority during 1953-57 in Peking's program to meet China's needs for skilled personnel; and during 1956-57, a government-established Scientific Planning Committee drafted an ambitious 12 year plan for development of the sciences covering the years 1956-67. By 1956 Peking claimed to have established 66 scientific research institutes under the national Academy of Sciences, with close to 5,000 researchers and students; 105 "scientific research centers," with over 10,000 researchers and technicians, under various government ministries; and numerous university research bodies.

There is no reason to doubt the abilities of Chinese to become qualified, or even outstanding, scientists and technicians, and Peking's adoption of the Soviet approach to the accelerated training of such persons will undoubtedly speed up the process of accumulating skilled personnel in these fields in China. But training, under any circumstances, takes time and costs money, and at the end of their first Plan period the Chinese Communists still had a long way to go in order to meet fully their needs for highly-qualified personnel.

Lack of experience and skill in economic planning created additional problems for the Peking regime during the first Plan period, and even with Soviet advisers, the Chinese Communists made some major and costly planning errors. Peking has subsequently admitted quite candidly that mistakes were made after the crop failures of 1953 and 1954 in underestimating development possibilities in 1955, and that development possibilities were overestimated in 1956, after the good crop year in 1955. The erratic course of industrialization during 1953-57 was due in part to these planning errors. In 1955, for example, when the Chinese Communists found they had unexpected surpluses of materials such as steel, cement, and timber on their hands, they began to dispose of surpluses by exporting them, and then they discovered in 1956 that they faced serious shortages of these same materials.

Many of the difficulties facing the Chinese Communists seemed to come to a head during 1956 and 1957. At the National Peoples Congress Meeting in June 1957, Premier Chou En-lai even admitted that, "Some people think that our first Five Year Plan has been completely bungled."

One fact was clear. During 1956, the Chinese Communists had over-expanded and overextended themselves in their economic program, and 1957 was of necessity a year of consolidation. In its initial plans for 1957, Peking made cuts in almost all key economic sectors. Compared to 1956, total national expenditures were cut back 4 percent. National defense expenditures were reduced 10 percent. "Capital construction" as a whole was reduced 21 percent. The planned increase in total industrial output was only 5 percent. Output of the machine-building industry was scheduled for a drop of 4 percent. No overall increase was planned for consumer goods production.

Economic difficulties undoubtedly were major contributary causes of restiveness and tensions within Communist China during 1957, a year in which there was a head-on clash between the Communist Party and the non-Communist intellectuals in China. In the spring of 1957, after Mao Tse-tung's famous speech on "contradictions," the Chinese Communists decided to encourage greater public expression of opinions on the part of China's intellectuals and students. The campaign to "let all flowers bloom and all schools of thought contend," which was first announced in 1956, blossomed forth in a surprising fashion in May of 1957. It was linked to a "rectification" campaign within the Communist Party, and the intellectuals were encouraged to express their criticism of the Party and its policies.

There are reasons to believe that one important factor impelling Peking's leaders to initiate this campaign was a growing feeling that rigid ideological controls were stifling the creativity of China's intellectual class, thereby hampering the nation's development program. The results of relaxing controls were startling, however, and many intellectuals began expressing bitter criticism of the regime and its policies, including its economic program. Soon the Communists were complaining that the campaign was producing too many "weeds" instead of "flowers," and after only one month of relatively free criticism, the Communists clamped down and counterattacked with a vigorous "anti-Rightist" campaign directed at the regime's most vocal critics.

The net result of the whole affair was to reveal that, despite repeated indoctrination, China's intellectuals had by no means been converted en masse to communism. The degree of hidden resentment and disaffection which was brought to light among important groups of intellectuals must have caused real distress to Peking's leaders. And instead of strengthening the bonds between the Chinese Communists and non-Communist intellectuals in China, the campaign probably intensified the tensions and frictions between them. This could mean that in the future Peking may have more rather than less difficulty in mobilizing the active support, and utilizing the skills, of this key group in China.

The problem of maintaining a minimum standard of living for the Chinese population also appeared to reach a difficult stage in 1957. Shortages of basic essentials became serious, and rationing had to be tightened. For the average person in China, 1957 was a year of belt-tightening, and Peking publicly admitted that some starvation took place, although it attributed this to bureaucratic bungling rather than to basic food shortages. The Chinese Communists' political power and control over the economy was never seriously threatened, however, as Peking amply and dramatically indicated when it adopted revolutionary new policies in 1958.

In late 1957, Peking's leaders, who have repeatedly demonstrated their capacity to learn from experience and to innovate and even gamble when faced with new problems, began to give evidence that they were rethinking many of their economic policies and were feeling their way toward important modifications of past policies. Their public statements indicated thinking along the following lines.

Investment in agriculture would be stepped up, with more emphasis being placed upon developing irrigation, reclamation, and output of chemical fertilizers. The transfer of land from food crops to industrial crops would be slowed down. Greater efforts would be made to develop the raw materials industries, as a means of improving domestic demand for commodities such as chemical fertilizers, coal, ferrous and nonferrous metals, petroleum, salt and soda, and to increase exports of coal, iron, salt, and nonferrous metals. An attempt would be made to reduce the proportion of agricultural goods in China's exports and to increase exports of raw materials and manufactured goods. Greater emphasis would be placed upon small-scale industries, requiring less capital investment and fewer imported machines, rather than large industrial plants. The level of technical and equipment standards in new industries would be lowered, and Chinese-made equipment would be used instead of imported equipment whenever possible, even if the former were more expensive and less efficient. Semimechanized and handicraft industries would receive greater attention. Somewhat less importance would be placed upon dispersion of industry in the interior of the country, and greater efforts would be made to utilize the productive capacity of existing industries in coastal areas. And some purely military factories would be converted to civilian production.

None of these proposals really prepared the people in China, however, for the revolutionary developments which were to take place during 1958, the initial year of China's second Five Year Plan. The "great leap forward," the massive drive to build small-scale industries and develop irrigation, and the radical "communization" program of 1958 introduced entirely new elements into the whole economic picture in Communist China. These are reviewed in the following chapter.

Chapter Seven

THE "LEAP FORWARD," INDUSTRIAL DECENTRALIZATION, AND COMMUNIZATION

Developments in Communist China since early 1958 have been so revolutionary and startling that it is impossible at this time to evaluate them with any sense of confidence, or to calculate with any accuracy what their long-range significance will be. Nineteen hundred and fifty-eight was the year of the "great leap forward," as Peking has described it, during which the Chinese Communists set immense goals for increased agricultural and industrial development, and claimed achievements which are incredible in the literal sense of the word. It was a year in which unprecedented development of small-scale industries and agricultural irrigation was claimed by Peking. And it was a year of communization, during which the Chinese Communists started carrying out the most radical political, economic, and social reorganization ever attempted in so short a time by a large nation.

It is difficult to take all the claims which Peking is now publicizing about the revolutionary events in Communist China during 1958 at face value, but, even if substantially discounted, they cannot be simply dismissed.

The Chinese Communists began 1958 by announcing that they were determined to achieve a "great leap forward" in their economy during the year and that they intended to catch up with Britain in the output (absolute, not per capita) of major industrial products after three five year plans -- or by 1972. Despite this self-confident statement of purpose, however, the actual targets which had been set in early 1958 for the year's output of various industrial and agricultural products, although they called for significant increases in production and an acceleration of economic growth after the slowdown of 1957, were, nonetheless, not inconsistent either with the Chinese Communists' past performance or with their overall planning as it had been earlier revealed.

As the year progressed, however, Peking threw away the book, so to speak, and repeatedly raised its targets. It began to project rates of development without any precedent in China or elsewhere. Finally, the Communists declared that it was their aim to double, in a single year, the output of almost every major industrial and agricultural product. To work toward these goals, during 1958 Peking fully mobilized China's millions, regimented them, and pressed them to labor for the state in an unprecedented way. And at the end of the year, despite a few admitted shortfalls, they claimed that most of these amazing targets had been achieved. Their claims are summarized in Table 4.

First of all, according to the Chinese Communists, they began in the fall of 1957 to mobilize tens of millions of people to make an unparalleled effort to develop new irrigation projects. Between October 1957 and June 1958, Peking now claims, over 100 million peasants were organized to build irrigation works which supplied water to 80 million additional acres

Table 4

Output of Principal Commodities 1957-59

| | 1957 | 1958 | | | 1959 |
	Claimed output	Initial target	Revised target	Claimed output	Initial target
Steel (million tons)	5.35	6.25	10.7	11	18
Coal (million tons)	128.6	150.7	300	270	380
Petroleum (million tons)	1.46	1.66	2.32	2.25	n.a.
Electricity (billion kwh)	19.0	22.5	27.5	27.5	n.a.
Grain (million tons)	185	196	350	375	525
Cotton (million tons)	1.64	1.75	3.50	3.32	5.0

of land -- raising the percentage of all cultivated land under irrigation from 31 percent in 1957, to 56 percent in mid-1958, and increasing the total of irrigated land in China to almost 150 million acres. The peasants were also mobilized to collect all available manure and to dredge mud from ponds to place on their fields. Immense quantities of manure were applied to the fields, Peking claimed. Both imports and domestic production of chemical fertilizers were stepped up. The goal for domestic fertilizer production in 1962 was set at 10 million tons, and Peking talked of an eventual production of 30 million tons. Deep plowing, close planting and other techniques new for China were vigorously pushed. State investments in agriculture were increased by 40 percent compared with 1957. Over a million party, government, and other urban workers were transferred to the countryside to participate in agriculture. And good weather gave a big boost to farm output.

There is no doubt that all of these factors contributed to a significant, and probably very sizable, spurt in agricultural production. But even taking all of them into consideration, it is virtually impossible to credit or support, on the basis of past experience anywhere in the world, the claims Peking has made. Apart from their overall claim that output of both grain and cotton has been doubled, the Chinese Communists claim that per acre yields have increased spectacularly; they say, for example, that the average per acre yield of wheat jumped 71 percent and rice 122 percent in 1958, as compared with 1957.

Peking's claims in the field of industry are only slightly less difficult to accept fully. Even though top priority was given to the steel and machine-building industries, the successive increases in the year's steel output target -- from 6.25 million tons early in the year to 7.1 million as of May, to 10.7 million as of August -- suggest a rate of development which has no precedent elsewhere. At the end of 1958, Peking claimed that during the year gross industrial output had increased 65 percent over 1957, and they asserted that steel production had reached 11 million tons.

One of the most important explanations for the remarkable spurt in overall industrial output claimed to have taken place during 1958, is to be found in the Chinese Communists' dramatic new program for developing small-scale industries throughout the breadth and width of China, in rural as well as urban areas. Decentralization of industry was begun by Peking even before 1958, but during 1958 the mobilization of local labor and resources to build small-scale enterprises was tremendous. Peking drew up standardized plans for small mines or factories producing everything from coal and steel to chemical fertilizers, and medium-size factories based upon these plans were built all over the country with local capital, labor, and resources.

A majority of the new "factories," however, were primitive -- actually they were little more than semihandicraft operations. Literally, hundreds of thousands of tiny "blast furnaces," for example, were built all over China, using local scrap or iron ore and coal. In late 1958, Peking claimed that over a million people were taking part in "steel" production; and Western visitors to China confirmed the fact that iron and steel of low quality, but good enough for the production of simple implements and utensils, were being produced day and night in primitive installations in villages and backyards all over the country. Although 1958's leap also involved faster development of large-scale modern industries, it was really the development of hundreds of thousands of small, labor-intensive, local industries which more than anything else accounted for the Chinese Communists' almost fantastic claims of increased overall industrial output.

The one development during 1958 which overshadowed all others, and raised the most questions for the future, was Peking's organization of China's rural population into so-called "people's communes." The first experimental commune was formed in China in April. The Chinese Communist Party Central Committee expanded the communization program on a nationwide basis in late August; and before the end of the year, the 740,000 collectives in China had for the most part been merged, on paper at least, into about 26,500 new communes.

The Chinese communes represent the most radical formula for reorganizing society ever attempted in the modern period, and they go far beyond anything tried so far on a nationwide basis in the Soviet Union. Ideologically and institutionally, they are interpreted by some as putting Communist China in the forefront of Communist experimentation.

Although, by early 1959, the Chinese Communists claimed that 99 percent of China's peasants had already been organized into communes formed by large-scale mergers of collective farms, it will clearly take some years for this "ultimate" form of social organization -- which Peking says will eventually provide the basis for a communist, as contrasted with a socialist, society -- to be consolidated. In the interim, many of the goals of communization remain on paper. There are wide differences in the actual organization and management of the new groups, and thousands of communes are still undergoing various stages of transition. But the aims of communization have already been clearly defined, and Peking claims to be making rapid progress in achieving them.

In essence, the communes in China are multipurpose units for the management of all agricultural, industrial, commercial, cultural, and military affairs in a given locality. Generally, a commune is established within the boundary of a _hsiang_ or township, and organizationally the _hsiang_ government and the commune are merged. Some early communes included only 2,000 or so households, but for the country as a whole they average slightly under 5,000 families per commune, and in many areas in China they now average between 5,000 and 10,000 families. Once organized, a commune takes over all property and common funds of the former collectives, and in time it absorbs almost all the privately-held plots, fruit trees, and domestic animals and fowl of its members, eliminating most of the last vestiges of private property. Commune members are eventually to be paid wages, plus rewards or bonuses for good performance and behavior; or to be put on the "wage-plus-supply" system, under which they receive rations of most necessities "free," and then are given a nominal wage in addition. All members of the commune, both men and women, are organized along military lines into work groups which can be used anywhere within the communes as needed. The commune is to develop a wide range of local industries, as well as promote increased agricultural output, and it should eventually achieve a fairly high degree of local self-sufficiency. Able-bodied men between 18 and 45 are liable for service in the commune's militia.

Perhaps the most revolutionary aspects of the communes are those affecting the social life of the people. Communal mess halls are being set up to replace private dining, and children are being placed in communal nurseries (which eventually, it is hoped, will be full-time boarding institutions). These mess halls and nurseries have apparently already been developed on a very large scale. By October 1958, for example, 310,000 mess halls were reported to be feeding over 70 percent of the population in one province, Honan.

In addition, the initial directive on communes authorized them to tear down private homes and use the materials to build new, relocated dwellings for the peasants. In a few places, the peasants are already living in such housing projects. In December 1958, however, a new party directive attempted to restrain excessive zeal by party members on the local level. It stated that under certain circumstances commune members will be allowed for some time to own their own homes, implements, and domestic animals, and to engage in domestic occupations that do not interfere with their collective labor. It also postponed communization in most urban areas.

One can only speculate about why the Chinese Communists decided to embark upon such a revolutionary program in 1958. They may have felt, after 1957, that their industrial and agricultural program was losing momentum, and that this justified drastic new measures. It is significant that both the collectivization of 1955 and the communization of 1958 followed relatively poor crop years, and were subsequently carried out at a rapid pace during periods when the prospects of good crops appeared to give the regime a margin for experimentation and error. It is possible that Peking's increasing difficulty from 1956 onward in importing the capital goods required for large-scale industries from the Soviet Union without receiving commensurate loans, may have led the Chinese Communists to decide that they should make greater efforts to achieve their goals through total mobilization of China's population for labor-intensive development projects in both agriculture and industry.

Political pressures in China, revealed more clearly than ever before during 1957, may have pushed Peking to take steps to strengthen its political control. And the inner logic of the Chinese Communists' revolutionary struggle, which has kept China in turmoil and off balance ever since 1949, may have driven Peking's leaders to keep moving ever faster toward their ultimate goal of a communist society.

Whatever Peking's motives for starting communization in 1958, it is obvious that if the Chinese Communists were to succeed in consolidating the communes, they would be able to control and direct the population and resources of the entire country to a remarkable degree. The available labor force would be greatly expanded, fully regimented, and transferable at will to different types of labor-intensive projects, both agricultural and industrial. In particular, women released from home duties would greatly increase the amount of available labor. Agricultural production could be further rationalized through planned use of land, large-scale development of public works, the introduction of new methods, and so on. Consumption could be further controlled -- for example, some mess halls reportedly have already reduced food consumption by 10 percent. Capital for investment, both local and national, could be more fully mobilized -- for example, it is estimated that some communes already are able to squeeze out as much as 20 to 30 percent more capital for investment than the collectives making them up were able to do.

The communes can, for all of these above-noted reasons, provide a stronger base than the collectives for Peking's decentralized industry drive. And the establishment of regimented, fairly self-sufficient, local units has great military significance in terms of China's defensive capabilities in time of war. The communes' social control over the population could provide a basis for nationwide birth control if Peking were to decide to limit its population growth -- at present, however, the Chinese Communists are talking more about labor shortages than about overpopulation.

While one can analyze the economic gains which Peking might achieve as a result of communization -- if it succeeds -- there is little doubt that this program, which involves an economic price in human terms, constitutes the biggest gamble made by Communist China to date. Even though there is almost no substantial evidence that China's peasants have so far been able to resist communization effectively, it is by no means certain how well the communes will work. They will involve huge administrative and immense human problems. The destruction of the family, the reduction of the individual to a cipher in a large social organization, and the almost superhuman demands for work placed upon the population might be more than even the long-suffering Chinese peasant will accept. Yet, this is not inevitable. The Chinese Communists have already demonstrated an ability to control, indoctrinate, and manipulate large masses of human beings to a remarkable degree, and they have already done many things which a decade ago would have seemed impossible in view of the traditional character of Chinese society. Their ability to embark on the communization program is a further demonstration of the totalitarian control which they now exercise in China.

As of early 1959, it is difficult not only to predict the future but even to evaluate the present. It seems prudent to reserve judgment on the claims Peking has made so far about increased agricultural and industrial output, since, in contrast to the economic statistics coming out of Communist China from 1954 through 1957, which had a fairly high degree of credibility, Peking's current overall claims are extremely difficult to justify on the basis either of information now available or of precedents elsewhere. One suspects that the Chinese Communists, for reasons not fully understandable, are now indulging in deliberate, large-scale falsification and manipulation of figures.

Even though it is necessary at present to reserve judgment on the precise magnitude of the accomplishments during 1958, there is, however, hardly any doubt that the Chinese Communists achieved a sizable spurt in the development of production during the year, and initiated new lines of policy of great importance for the future. They clearly raised agricultural output significantly, partly as a result of what they were able to achieve through using mobilized labor for public works and by applying a few simple improvements in agricultural methods on a wide scale, and partly as a result of good weather. Although the evidence is still inconclusive -- and will remain so until concrete results, such as more liberal food rations in China or increased exports abroad, become apparent 1/ -- it is conceivable that Peking has made a jump forward in agriculture which could greatly ease, for the time being at least, the economic strains and pressures which the lag in agriculture created in the past.

The dramatic program for building small-scale industries has clearly added much to Peking's capacity for industrial growth. It is quite likely that, in time, many of these industries will prove to be uneconomic or impractical. But, in the meantime, there is little doubt that the Chinese Communists can achieve significant additions to output to supplement their construction of large-scale modern plants, by increased utilization of local labor, capital, and resources for decentralized industry, and it is likely that small industries will continue to play an important role in Chinese development. By the end of 1958, there were indications, however, that the developments in China during the previous year had created many dislocations in the Chinese economy. It is still too early to judge what the future effects of these dislocations will be.

The biggest question mark for the future is raised by the communes. If they succeed, great opportunities for accelerated development may be opened up for the Peking regime. If the Chinese people refuse to accept them in the long run, the communes could prove to be a great mistake which could have a very adverse affect upon every aspect of the Chinese Communists' program.

PART II

FOREIGN ECONOMIC RELATIONS

Chapter Eight

OVERALL AND SOVIET BLOC TRADE

As Communist China's development program has progressed, Peking's capacity and need to engage in foreign trade has increased significantly and the volume of China's trade rose steadily during the first Plan period until 1957, when domestic economic difficulties in China caused it to drop temporarily. Industrialization under Communist China's Five Year Plan required large amounts of imported capital goods, equipment, and raw materials, and to pay for needed imports the Chinese Communists had to export an increasing volume of agricultural and other products. Accompanying the overall growth in China's foreign trade, a radical change took place in the direction of Chinese trade, as the Communists reoriented China's economy away from the West and toward the Communist bloc. The composition of the trade underwent significant changes as well. 1/

The rise of China's foreign trade from 1950 onward is shown in Table 5.

Table 5

Foreign Trade 1950-57
($ billion)

	Imports	Exports	Total trade turnover
1950	0.90	0.86	1.76
1952	1.59	1.15	2.74
1953	1.95	1.47	3.43
1954	1.86	1.72	3.58
1955	2.56	2.10	4.66
1956	2.24	2.35	4.59
1957	2.02	2.28	4.30

The increase in total trade -- about 57 percent during the first Plan period -- was substantial, but uneven. There were big spurts in 1953 and 1955, followed by declines in 1956 and 1957. Exports increased more than imports, but serious economic difficulties and overexpansion within China in 1956 forced a cutback in exports along with imports in 1957.

For 1958, the Chinese projected a figure of $4.67 billion, and late in 1958 Peking claimed that this target would be exceeded by over $230 million.

The overall foreign trade level during recent years, amounting to between $4 billion and $4.5 billion annually, is undoubtedly considerably higher than the level of China's prewar trade, although it is difficult to make exact comparisons because of the large price rises since the mid-1930s. By 1956, China's total trade in per capita terms amounted to approximately $7 per person, and it represented roughly 11 percent of China's 1956 national income.

From 1950 through 1955, the Chinese Communists consistently had an adverse balance in overall commodity trade, despite claims to the contrary. Total imports exceeded total exports by between $400 million and $500 million in most years (except 1950 and 1954 when the gap was smaller), and the difference was made up by receipts from foreign loans, overseas Chinese remittances, expenditures by foreigners in China (Soviet citizens, for the most part), and the like. As receipts from foreign loans steadily declined and repayments fell due, however, this situation changed. In 1956, China had an export surplus of $115 million and, in 1957, the export surplus increased to $261 million.

At present, the level of Chinese Communist imports of items essential to industrialization and economic development depends primarily on China's capacity to export; this has led Peking's leaders to make extraordinary efforts to maximize exports, even at great sacrifice to consumers in China. According to Yeh Chi-chuang, Minister of Foreign Trade, the Chinese Communist Party Central Committee and the State Council in Peking laid down a policy in 1954 which in effect gives clear priority to exports over domestic consumption. According to this policy, "commodities that are not essential to the livelihood of the people" should be exported in "as large a quantity as possible" with the "surplus [i.e. after exports] for domestic sales."

Other commodities which are more important to consumers in China "but short of an urgent demand on the domestic market" should be "reduced in domestic sales to make a bigger export possible." Only for such absolutely vital commodities as grains and vegetable oils which are "essential to the livelihood of the people and of which a short supply exists in the domestic market" should exports be limited by quotas. In this third category the Chinese Communists have set quotas, but the quotas have been large enough to allow sizable exports even of rationed commodities in short supply within China such as food grains, pork, vegetable oils, and cotton cloth.

One of the most striking aspects of Communist China's foreign trade pattern compared to prewar Chinese trade has been the revolutionary change in the direction of China's trade. Before World War II, China traded largely with the West and Japan. Prewar trade with the Soviet Union amounted to 1 percent or less of China's total trade, and trade with Eastern European countries was even less. Soon after 1949, however, the Chinese Communists deliberately redirected trade toward the Communist bloc, as is shown in Table 6 (see also Appendix Table 8).

At the start, most of the Soviet bloc trade was with the Soviet Union, but the Satellites' trade with China has steadily grown in importance.

Table 6

Share of Communist China's Total Trade
with the Communist Bloc
(percent)

1950	34
1951	63
1952	78
1953	78
1954	80
1955	82
1956	75
1957	75 (preliminary estimate)

When China's first Five Year Plan got underway in 1953, of the 75 percent of Communist China's total trade which was with the Communist bloc, about 56 percent was with the USSR, 17 percent with Eastern European Communist states, and 3 percent with Asian Communist states. By 1957, however, Communist China's trade with the USSR was about 50 percent of China's total foreign trade, while trade with the other Communist countries was roughly 25 percent. Preliminary reports from Peking on China's trade during 1958 indicate that the Soviet Union accounted for only 40 percent; whether or not the Satellites' share went up proportionately is not yet clear.

Chinese Communist statistics in yuan figures when converted into dollars, indicate that Peking's trade with the Communist bloc as a whole increased from $.59 billion in 1950 to $2.14 billion in 1952, to a peak of $3.8 billion in 1955, before dropping to $3.5 billion in 1956.

There are puzzling differences in Chinese and Soviet figures, however. The Chinese Communists, in publishing Soviet ruble figures on trade between China and the USSR alone, state that 1956 trade was 6.99 billion rubles, or $1.75 billion at official exchange rates. These figures, and published percentages on the relative value of Soviet and Satellite trade, would indicate that total Communist China-bloc trade was only $2.68 billion in 1956, a figure considerably below the one which Chinese yuan figures indicate ($3.5 billion). Soviet sources have published a figure of 5.99 billion rubles or $1.50 billion, for Sino-Soviet trade in 1956, indicating an even smaller total Communist China-bloc trade of $2.25 billion.

It is difficult to explain these discrepancies. Possibly, some important elements in Sino-Soviet trade, in particular Soviet exports of military equipment to China and Chinese payments for them, may be excluded from the ruble figures. Or, possibly, the discrepancies arise partly because of the difficulty of converting such figures into U. S. dollars at official exchange rates when in fact the figures represent barter transactions, and little is know about pricing practices in Sino-Soviet barter arrangements. Also, differences in exchange rates may result in overstatement of the value of Communist China's trade with the Soviet bloc in relation to China's total trade.

Soviet figures indicate, in any case, that in 1956 Communist China accounted for over one fifth of the Soviet Union's total trade and ranked at the top of Moscow's trading partners in that year, surpassing even East Germany, Czechoslovakia, and Poland in importance. Since 1956, however, significant new trends have appeared in Peking's trade with the Soviet bloc. While Peking's trade with East Europe has steadily risen, Communist China's trade with the Russians declined in 1957, and the Chinese have found it necessary to maintain a large export surplus in Sino-Soviet trade.

According to Soviet statistics, trade between Communist China and the USSR dropped to $1.28 billion in 1957. Of this total, Peking's exports accounted for $738 million, while its imports from the Russians were only $544 million. The Chinese Communists, in short, presumably had to maintain an export surplus in trade with the USSR of almost $200 million in order to repay past Soviet loans. Soviet trade with China contrasted sharply with Soviet-East Europe trade, in which the Russians, due to increasing economic demands in the Satellites, had a large export surplus exceeding $600 million.

Chinese Communist statements in the fall of 1958 suggested that Peking's export surplus in trade with the USSR is still growing. It was reported that Communist China expected exports to the Soviet Union in 1958 to be 23 percent over 1957, while imports were expected to rise by only 12 percent. These percentages suggest that Sino-Soviet trade in 1958 may total (in figures comparable to those in the preceding paragraph derived from ruble figures) about $1.5 billion -- Chinese exports amounting to $900 million and imports to $600 million -- Peking's export surplus therefore totaling about $300 million.

The composition of trade between China and USSR is revealed by other figures which Peking has published on this trade during 1956. These figures, summarized in Table 7, show the trade to have consisted primarily of an exchange of Chinese agricultural products and raw materials for Soviet industrial capital goods.

Table 7

Sino-Soviet Trade: Commodity Composition 1956
(percent)

Chinese Exports		Soviet Exports	
Foodstuffs	40	Machinery and equipment	71
Nonferrous and rare metals	16	Petroleum products	12
Textiles	12	Ferrous metals	8
Textile raw materials	8	Other	9
Animal by-products	3		
Other	21		
	100		100

Although the 1950-51 Western restrictions on trade with Communist China, resulting from the Korean conflict, were one factor reinforcing the Chinese trend toward trading with Soviet bloc countries, there are many reasons to believe that they were not the basic cause. The Chinese Communists began to "lean to one side" even before the fighting in Korea, and numerous barter and other economic agreements made with the Soviet bloc resulted in a maximum trade integration. Furthermore, despite the changing character of Sino-Soviet economic relations -- that is, the falling off of Soviet credits and the growth of China's export surpluses -- in some respects, Peking's economic integration with the USSR and the whole bloc appears still to be increasing, rather than decreasing.

To cite a few examples of increasing links, Sino-Soviet cooperation in joint exploitation of the Amur River Valley, based upon a 1956 agreement, has steadily developed; and, in 1958, Peking not only agreed to strengthen cooperation with the USSR and European Communist states belonging to the Mutual Economic Assistance Council, but also signed long-term rather than one year trade agreements with several of the Satellites. By the end of 1958, it had signed long-term trade agreements with Bulgaria, Poland, Hungary, Rumania, and North Korea. In 1958, also, the Russians revealed that they were permitting a sizable lag in Chinese barter deliveries to the Soviet Union. They indicated that discussion of payments problems is not initiated until Communist China is more than $75 million behind in its deliveries, and they claimed that to help Peking they had even reduced domestic Russian output of certain commodities by 2 to 3 percent to facilitate absorption of exports from China.

The Chinese Communists have obtained important advantages from their barter arrangements with other Communist nations, including assured sources of supply for needed materials, but there have been disadvantages too. For one thing, the Chinese have limited their own economic maneuverability and placed themselves in a fairly dependent position vis-à-vis the Soviet bloc. In addition, there is some evidence that due to high transport costs and possibly also to the Russians' superior bargaining position, China's trade with the Soviet bloc may have involved relatively poor terms of trade. The Chinese Minister of Foreign Trade has stated that with the exception of "some necessary readjustments," the prices of commodities exchanged in Sino-Soviet trade in 1957 were the same as prices established in the original Sino-Soviet trade agreement in 1950, and although it is difficult to compute and balance the many price changes which have taken place on the international market since 1950, Peking has been vague and defensive about how the maintenance of fixed prices in Sino-Soviet trade has affected China's interests.

A comparison of Soviet and Chinese figures on the value of Sino-Soviet trade suggests that the exchange rate actually used in this trade may be one which favors the Soviet Union considerably. Studies of available data on the prices of Soviet goods offered for sale on the domestic China market indicate some wide discrepancies between these prices and those of goods which the Chinese Communists could buy in Hong Kong. Evidence of this sort is not conclusive, but it is at least suggestive.

The slight reversal for the first time in 1956 of the trend toward increasing Chinese trade dependence upon the Soviet bloc could be an important straw in the wind for the future. Although it seems highly probable that as long as China's entire economic program is linked to the Soviet bloc -- as it has been to date -- a large majority of Peking's trade will be with the bloc countries; it is nonetheless possible that China at some point may decide to increase the proportion of its trade with the free world.

The commodity composition of China's overall foreign trade has also undergone important changes during the past eight years of Communist rule. The Peking regime has cut consumer goods imports to a minimum and has attempted to reserve its foreign exchange resources as much as possible for imports of machinery and raw materials required for industrialization. The pattern of exports has not changed so much. As in prewar days, China's exports still consist largely of agricultural products. However, the Chinese Communists have become net exporters of some items, such as grain, of which China used to have an import surplus, and they are now attempting to increase exports of various types of manufactured goods on a sizable scale.

Although Peking had not published, at the time of writing, any detailed commodity breakdown of foreign trade since 1950, it had made a few general statements which give a general picture of the character of its trade. These various Chinese statements indicate that during the first Five Year Plan period about 60 percent of Communist China's total imports consisted of "machines and equipment" (as used here, this category is very broadly defined, and probably includes imports of military equipment, since the specific figures the Chinese Communists have released on machinery and equipment imports do not add up to 60 percent of total trade); 30 percent were basic raw materials for industry and agriculture, of which metals made up approximately one third; and the remaining 10 percent were made up of consumer goods.

If these percentages are correct, they would indicate that in very rough terms Communist China imported annually, during the first Five Year Plan period, an average of about $1.2 billion of "producer's goods" of all sorts (probably including military equipment); about $600 million of raw materials, of which roughly $200 million consisted of metals; and about $200 million of consumer goods. Published Soviet figures, however, indicate not only smaller overall quantities but also a smaller percentage of machines, equipment, and other capital goods. Among the most important capital goods imports have been industrial machinery and equipment, transportation equipment including railway cars, trucks, machine tools, and tractors. Major materials imports have included steel, nonferrous metals, petroleum, fertilizers, cotton, rubber, dyestuffs, and chemicals. Items such as drugs, kerosene, and sugar have been important among consumer goods imports.

The Chinese Communists state that in overall terms, during recent years, about 75 percent of their exports have consisted of agricultural commodities and agricultural processed goods, and 25 percent of mineral products and manufactured goods. In very rough terms, these percentages represent about $1.5 billion of agricultural products and $500 million of other goods exported per year. China's traditional export products have consisted of a wide variety of commodities, and these still make up the bulk of Chinese exports. They include: soya beans, miscellaneous food products, tung oil, various types of vegetable oils, eggs and other dairy products, animals and animal products, hog bristles, silk, tea, coal, iron ore, tin, tungsten, antimony, manganese and other mineral products, handicrafts, and many miscellaneous products such as fiber goods, straw, braid, human hair, hairnets, and so on. Under the Communists, grain and pork have increased in importance as exports, and recently the Chinese have begun to export manufactured products of modern industry in sufficient quantities to offer very serious competition to Japan in Southeast Asia.

An examination of available details on a number of key imports and export items in Communist China's trade gives a somewhat clearer picture of overall Chinese trade, and its relation to the Chinese economy as a whole. The importance of capital goods imports to Communist China's Five Year Plan is revealed by an official Chinese Communist statement indicating that China was only able to produce 60 percent of its needs for all kinds of machinery and equipment during 1953-57, and therefore had to fill 40 percent of its needs by imports, almost wholly from the Soviet bloc. Peking has also stated that 38 percent of China's total "capital construction expenditures" during the first Five Year Plan was for machinery and equipment. These two statements would seem to indicate that during 1953-57, Communist China's machinery and equipment requirements for projects included in the Five Year Plan amounted to roughly $5.88 billion, and that of this total it was necessary to import approximately $2.35 billion, averaging perhaps slightly under $500 million of machinery and equipment per year.

This rough figure may exaggerate the facts; Soviet statistics indicate that Russian exports of equipment and machinery -- not including military equipment -- to China rose from $163 million in 1953 to only $305 million in 1956. Most of this came from the Soviet bloc and probably a majority was devoted to the Soviet aid projects in China. Since less than 60 of these projects were completed during the first Five Year Plan, furthermore, it is likely that machinery and equipment imports from the Soviet bloc will have to continue at a fairly high level. 2/

The Chinese Communists have asserted recently, however, that they would like to avoid increasing the proportion of these imports in China's total import trade, and will try to do this by lowering standards of machinery and equipment requirements in planned industrial expansion so that Chinese industry can supply a larger percentage of China's needs. They hope to reduce their imports of machinery and equipment to 30 percent of China's total needs during the second Plan period. During 1957, when Communist China's balance of payments situation became increasingly difficult, top Chinese Communist leaders stated that in the future they should only import machinery and equipment which cannot be made in China and should use Chinese-made machinery whenever possible.

As Communist China's own heavy industry developed during the first Plan period, the proportion of key import items as a percentage of Chinese total supply of these items was steadily reduced between 1953 and 1956, according to official Chinese claims. Imports of rolling and forging equipment reportedly dropped from 32 to 28 percent, and imports of lathes from 36 to 24 percent. An average of 22 percent of China's total needs for transformers was imported over the four years, but by 1956 the figure was claimed to be only 15 percent.

During the first four years of the Five Year Plan, Communist China probably produced roughly 72,000 machine tools itself, and it imported almost 22,000. During this same period, when China built its first automotive plant, it produced fewer than 2,000 trucks, while it imported 40,000. Imports between 1953 and 1956 also included 1,400 mining drills, almost 1,600 railway cars, and roughly 16,000 tractors. These figures are indicative of the fact that China is still very dependent upon capital goods imports for further development; but this dependence may decline steadily in the future.

Iron and steel have also been important imports during the past few years and although China's own production has risen, so have its needs. China's own steel output totaled 11 to 12 million tons during the four year period of 1953-56. According to one set of statistics, during this same period China's total imports of steel were 2.87 million tons, averaging roughly 700,000 tons a year, but dropping from 852,000 tons in 1953 to 608,000 tons in 1956. Another slightly different set of statistics in percentage form indicates a drop in the share of imported steel from 36 percent in 1953 to 14 percent in 1956. It seems likely that at least for some years Communist China will continue to find it necessary to import several hundred thousand tons of steel a year, including specialized alloy steels, even though the Chinese have stated that they hope by the end of the second Five Year Plan to be able to produce close to 100 percent of their own steel needs.

Petroleum is another vital product which the Chinese Communists have had to import in significant quantities, and exclusively from the Soviet bloc because of Western trade restrictions. During 1953-56, Communist China imported about 5 million tons from both the USSR and Eastern Europe. When viewed in the perspective of world consumption of petroleum this seems a small amount, but it nonetheless provided over half of China's needs during that period, since Chinese domestic production totaled only 3.5 million tons over these four years. Although the Chinese Communists are attempting to develop their own petroleum industry, Chinese needs for petroleum may well increase even more rapidly than domestic output, and there is every reason to expect that petroleum will continue to be a major import item.

Nonferrous metals such as copper and aluminum have also been imports of considerable importance, although Communist China's effort to push its own production of nonferrous metals has apparently decreased its dependence upon imports in this field. According to one Chinese Communist claim, imports of nonferrous metals supplied 38 percent of China's needs in 1953, but only 8 percent in 1956. At another point, Peking has stated that by 1956 imports of nonferrous metals had totaled 290,000 tons, but it is not clear whether this figure covers 1950-56, or only 1953-56. Although China is well endowed with resources of tin, antimony, tungsten, and manganese, the copper output is relatively small (although it is now being rapidly developed), and the aluminum industry is still in its infancy (the first Five Year Plan target for 1957 production was only 20,000 tons). Accordingly, imports of metals may continue to be vital to Communist China for some time to come.

Three other very important imports during the first Five Year Plan period -- which in contrast with the commodities discussed so far, came to a large extent from the free world rather than from the Soviet bloc -- were chemical fertilizers, cotton, and rubber.

During the first four years of the Plan period, Communist China imported almost 1.4 million tons of chemical fertilizers, and by 1956 this was the largest item among Peking's imports from the non-Communist world, reflecting a growing recognition by Peking of the necessity of investing more in agriculture. These imports rose from 5,000 tons in 1953 to 710,000 tons in 1956. Whereas, in 1953, Communist China imported only 2 percent of the small total of chemical fertilizer which it used, in 1956 the figure was 67 percent. Because present plans to expand fertilizer production in China will take time to fulfill, a high level of fertilizer imports will probably continue.

Although the Chinese Communists claimed not long after coming to power in 1949, that they had achieved self-sufficiency in cotton, in actual fact the rising demands of their textile industry and the fluctuations in domestic cotton output forced them to import cotton on a significant scale, particularly during poor crop years. Peking has reported total cotton imports at 451,000 tons during 1950-56. In 1950-51, the Chinese Communists imported 195,000 tons, in large part from the United States, but thereafter, as a result of the American embargo, Pakistan became the main source, supplying China with 200,000 tons over a seven year period. Other important suppliers have included Egypt, India, Sudan, Burma, Mexico, and Brazil. Recently, Egypt has become especially important to China as a source of cotton. Cotton imports, however, have made up only a relatively small proportion of China's total mill consumption, which averaged over a million tons a year in 1953-56, and the good Chinese cotton crop of 1957-58 (a record crop of nearly 3.5 million tons, double that of 1957, was claimed for 1958) could cause a decline in future imports.

Communist China's rubber imports during the first Five Year Plan period were sizable. Peking obtained 50,000 tons annually from Ceylon paying for it largely with rice, and it purchased smaller quantities elsewhere. The Chinese hope to develop rubber production in South China, but large-scale rubber imports are likely to continue if the present interruption of Peking's trade with these areas is ended.

If information on Communist China's imports is spotty, detailed information on its overall exports is even more difficult to obtain. The wide range of commodities of agricultural origin which make up the bulk of the export trade are so varied that only a few items individually constitute big exports in terms of value. Some data are available, however, on a few important export commodities, including grain and pork, which are of special interest because exports of these items compete so directly with unsatisfied domestic consumption demands.

The Chinese Communists have stated that exports of grain totaled 4.02 million tons in the four year period 1953-56, amounting to an average of roughly 1 million tons per year. These figures include only grain as such, including rice and wheat, but not including soya beans or potatoes which formerly were included in Peking's statistics of domestic "grain" production. Grain exports reached a peak of 1.32 million tons in 1956, and then the stringent food situation within China, partly caused by natural disasters in 1956, led Peking to make a drastic cut in the export quota for 1957, lowering exports to 780,000 tons, a reduction of 540,000 tons from the previous year.

In terms of China's total grain output, exports during the first Five Year Plan period did not constitute a large portion of China's output. They probably did not exceed, in fact, roughly 1 to 2 percent of China's total production. But for a country compelled to institute nationwide grain rationing at a low level, achieving even this volume of exports involved very real sacrifice by the population. Peking has been determined to earn foreign exchange in every possible way, however, and if, for purposes of very rough calculation, one figures the value of a ton of grain in foreign trade at $100, then Communist China has been earning perhaps $100 million a year from these exports, or over 5 percent of her export earnings -- a significant figure. Grain exports have played an important role not only in Communist China's trade with the Soviet bloc, but also in trade with the free world. The Chinese exported 270,000 tons of rice a year to Ceylon alone, during much of the first Plan period. 3/

In addition to food grains, soya beans have also been an important Chinese Communist export item. Although China, before Communist rule, was a net importer of grain, it has traditionally been a large exporter of soya beans. During recent years, the Chinese Communists have been maintaining shipments of about a million tons of soya beans a year. It is still below the prewar level, however.

Exports of pork, like grain exports, have had a directly adverse effect on the Chinese consumer, since pork is the most important meat constituent in the Chinese diet, and output has lagged far behind both plans and domestic needs. Despite the domestic pork shortage in China which finally led to nationwide rationing in 1957, exports of pigs and pork averaged well over 100,000 tons a year, during the entire first Plan period, reaching a peak in 1955 and 1956. As in the case of grain, however, the Chinese Communists were forced to cut exports drastically in 1957; in mid-year they said that pork exports would be cut by one half, from 162,000 tons in 1956 to 77,000 in 1957.

Very little detailed data are available on the overall export level of the myriad other agricultural products, such as tung oil, hog bristles, eggs, silk, vegetable oils, and so on, which make up China's export trade, although there is every evidence that Chinese Communists are pushing exports of all these items as much as they can.

Special metals have traditionally been another Chinese export item of considerable significance, and the bulk of Communist China's exports of nonferrous metals, such as tin, antimony, tungsten, and manganese, has been going to the Soviet bloc. In one statement, Peking has claimed that in the four year period 1953-56, these exports totaled 19,000 tons, rising to a figure close to 9,500 tons in 1956. They may actually have been considerably larger than this, however. Soviet statistics indicate that in 1956, Russia alone imported 15,700 tons of tin, 4,700 tons of alumina, 7,000 tons of antimony, and 10,500 tons of smelted nonferrous metals from China. Furthermore, the strategic importance of these metals is greater than it appears from the tonnage figures.

Of all the developments in Communist China's export pattern during the past few years, one of the most significant, particularly in its potentialities for future economic competition between the Communist bloc and the West, has been the increase in exports of manufactured industrial products. To date, these exports still constitute only a relatively small percentage of Communist China's overall trade, but the trend is one of great potential significance for the future. Communist China's capacity to develop exports of manufactured goods has steadily increased as industrialization has developed, and the Chinese Communists are now exporting not only consumer goods but also some capital goods, to both Soviet bloc and free world countries. These exports include sizable amounts of cotton textiles, machinery for factories, and even steel.

In 1957, one Chinese Communist publication stated that China's exports of cotton cloth have amounted to about 600 million yards annually in recent years. This figure -- which, if correct, would mean that Peking has been exporting about 10 percent of its cloth output -- may be an exaggeration; but it is a fact that during a period of severe domestic shortage and rationing, Peking has exported large quantities of textiles in order to meet its export commitments to Soviet bloc countries and to compete for free world markets in Southeast Asia and elsewhere in order to earn foreign exchange. Communist China's exports of other consumer goods, a large percentage of them to Southeast Asia, now include a wide range of items including bicycles, enamelware, fountain pens, cigarettes, and sewing machines. The Chinese have also been exporting various types of machinery and equipment, including entire textile mills and other plants, both in its foreign aid programs (to be discussed below) and in its normal foreign trade with countries in the free world as well as in the Soviet bloc. Peking has also stated that during 1953-56, Communist China's steel exports totaled 320,000 tons, 200,000 of this being exported in 1956. And, in 1956, it exported about a half million tons of pig iron to the USSR alone.

Reviewing Communist China's overall foreign trade during its first Five Year Plan, the total volume of trade increased greatly over the five years, but as the Plan period drew to a close it leveled off -- partly as a result of domestic economic difficulties -- and it seems probable that increases in total trade may be more gradual in the future than in the past few years. As industrialization developed during the first Five Year Plan, China's need for imports of essential machinery, equipment, and raw materials rose steadily, and consequently Peking pushed exports very hard. The cutback in some agricultural exports in 1957 indicated, however, that Peking was encountering difficulty in expanding its traditional exports.

The Chinese Communists' response to their tight economic and trade situation in 1957 was to propose two major trends in trade for the future. First of all, as stated before, they proposed to set limits upon the future import of machinery and equipment and to make strenuous efforts to meet more of China's own needs for capital goods from domestic production. Secondly, they proposed to increase exports of both manufactured goods and raw materials relative to their exports of agricultural products. During 1958 the results of this policy began to be apparent, particularly in Southeast Asia. And exports of manufactured or processed goods to the Communist bloc have also increased.

Precise prediction of how much Peking can achieve along these lines is difficult. Undoubtedly, Communist China's own output of capital goods will continue to rise, and this could make possible some reduction in the imports of these items from the Soviet bloc, or perhaps some increase in the Chinese exports to the free world. And Peking's current development of small-scale industries may have the effect of reducing Communist China's needs for imported capital goods relative to its overall program of industrial expansion. On the other hand, if a rapid pace of industrial development in China is maintained, it seems probable that a continuing high level of capital goods imports will be required for the development of large-scale modern industries. For one thing, roughly two thirds of the Soviet aid projects promised to China during the first Plan period remain to be completed, and the new projects recently announced for the second Plan period are just being started; and most of these projects will certainly require large-scale imports of capital goods.

In the field of manufactured consumer goods, the precarious supply-demand situation domestically will undoubtedly continue to impose limitations on the possibilities of expanding exports. Nonetheless, Peking has clearly indicated in the past few years that it is willing and able to export sizable quantities of items such as cotton textiles even though they are in short supply within China. Also, output appeared to increase substantially in 1958, and is slated to grow even more in 1959. And it is certainly possible that the Chinese Communists will continue and even substantially increase exports of this sort. Decisions on what to export are often politically determined in a Communist country, and China's level of textile and other consumer goods exports may depend less, therefore, upon the real needs of the Chinese population than upon Peking's estimate of how successfully it can maintain the domestic rationing system without creating serious internal tensions.

Of course, if the Chinese Communists decide to increase investments in consumer goods industries to speed up their development, the amounts of such goods available for export could certainly be increased rapidly. Exports of consumer goods which are not absolutely essential to minimum living standards in China, such as bicycles and pens, can be definitely increased if Peking decides to step up output of them. Although final statistics on free world trade with Communist China in 1958 are not yet available at the time of writing, there is evidence that Peking's exports of manufactured goods to non-Communist areas increased substantially during 1958. In early 1959, a sharp drop took place in Peking's exports to some free world nations, possibly as a result of dislocations within China after the communization program; but there is little basis for believing at present that this drop will be more than temporary.

Communist China's long-run potential to increase exports of raw materials such as coal, and to a lesser extent iron ore, is considerable. China has sizable deposits, and production has been steadily rising. During Peking's first Plan period, however, the volume of exports in this category was definitely limited by the supply and demand situation within China. China's own domestic requirements for basic raw materials increased greatly as a result of industrialization and in 1957 Peking admitted that output of raw materials had lagged behind the development of other heavy industries. At the start of 1958 there was no doubt that the domestic supply situation for coal and iron was very tight. And the rapid development projected for steel and other heavy industries in China indicates that internal requirements for these raw materials will continue to rise rapidly.

It is estimated that in recent years Communist China has been exporting perhaps a million or more tons of coal and several hundred thousand tons of iron ore annually, but these figures are not large in terms of China's total trade. Peking's ability to export iron ore will probably improve, however, with the completion of work now going on at the high-grade iron mines on Hainan Island -- these mines exported over a million tons of ore annually to Japan during World War II, and they are capable of producing more if further developed -- and the rapid development of new coal mines on the mainland of China will probably also improve Peking's export capacity.

The one prediction that can be made with confidence is that Communist China will continue its efforts to expand overall foreign trade. It seems probable that trade expansion will be more difficult, and consequently somewhat slower, in the future than in the immediate past. But developments in China during 1958 introduce a large element of uncertainty about the future and, conceivably, Peking may find it possible to increase exports at a more rapid rate than seemed likely at the end of China's first Plan period.

Chapter Nine

CHINA'S TRADE WITH THE FREE WORLD

As Communist China's industrialization program has developed, and as its overall foreign trade has risen, Chinese Communist trade with free world countries has also increased steadily. Since 1952, Peking's leaders have actively fostered trade with numerous countries outside of the Communist bloc, and although almost four fifths of Communist China's overall foreign trade during the first Five Year Plan period was with Soviet bloc countries, Peking's trade with countries outside the bloc rose significantly during the same period. By the end of the Plan period it was close to its pre-1949 level. This trade between Communist China and the free world, especially as it affects Asia, is already a factor of major importance in the general economic competition between the Communists and the West, and it could become even more important in the future. Economic and political motives are closely interwoven in Peking's whole foreign economic policy, and therefore the growth of Chinese Communist trade with the free world has important political as well as economic implications.

Communist China's efforts actively to promote trade outside of the Soviet bloc began at about the time of the Moscow economic conference convened by the Russians in 1952. At that conference, Chinese Communist representatives signed so-called "trade agreements" with groups of private businessmen from 11 non-Communist countries, including Great Britain, France, West Germany, Belgium, Netherlands, Switzerland, and Italy. Although these "agreements" were in many respects merely propaganda documents, incapable of being fulfilled because of existing Western restrictions on China trade, they symbolized Peking's desire to undermine the existing restrictions and to develop trade relations with the West.

Western restrictions on trade with Communist China steadily decreased in the course of the first Plan period. These special restrictions had grown out of the Korean conflict. After Peking's intervention in North Korea, the United States had taken the lead in imposing economic warfare measures against Communist China by placing a complete embargo on China trade, and following a UN resolution calling for restrictions on trade with China, many other countries had forbidden trade with the Chinese Communists in a very wide range of goods classified as strategic. Until the 1953 truce in Korea, there was fairly general agreement about enforcement of the controls on China trade, but after 1953 pressure for relaxing the controls grew in many non-Communist countries, including Great Britain and Japan. In a gradual process, these countries eased restrictions by removing the strategic classification from many items, until in mid-1957 there was a general relaxation by most major trading countries other than the United States. By the end of 1957, the controls on China trade, other than those imposed by the United States, were in general limited to those applied by Western nations to trade with all Soviet bloc countries in goods having a direct military significance.

The Chinese Communists also began to increase their efforts to promote trade with various Asian countries in 1952. In 1951, they had signed trade contracts with the Indians, and in June 1952, they signed a "trade agreement" with a Japanese business group calling for £30 million trade each way. An important trade pact was concluded in late 1952 with the government of Ceylon; this five year agreement on the exchange of Chinese rice for Ceylonese rubber created a very serious gap in Western trade restriction against Peking. In 1953, China signed another trade agreement, this time with Indonesia. This was followed by further trade agreements with India and Burma in 1954, and then by numerous other agreements. By early 1959, Communist China had concluded intergovernmental trade agreements not only with 12 Communist states, but also with 19 non-Communist governments -- India, Afghanistan, Ceylon, Burma, Indonesia, Cambodia, the United Arab Republic (both Egypt and Syria), Lebanon, Finland, Sweden, Denmark, Norway, Nepal, Yemen, Tunisia, Morocco, Sudan, and Iraq. And altogether over 90 non-Communist countries or areas were trading with Communist China in 1958.

Major limits on how far Communist China could go in actually expanding trade outside the Communist bloc have been imposed, however, not only by the Western trade restrictions but also by the integration of China's economy and foreign trade with the Soviet bloc. The fact that a large percentage of China's export capacity and foreign exchange has been definitely committed to pay for imports from the Soviet bloc was one of the reasons why relaxation of Western trade restrictions in 1957 did not result in any sudden, large jump in Communist China's trade with the West -- to the disappointment of many of those who had been most vocal in calling for a lifting of the restrictions. Until the end of 1955, in fact, the increase of Communist China's trade with the free world was not as rapid as the rise in its trade with the Soviet bloc; but in 1956, for the first time, China's free world trade increased relative to its bloc trade.

There are different estimates of Communist China's total trade with the free world. Estimates based upon official Chinese Communist figures indicate that this trade amounted to roughly $1.17 billion in 1950, dropped to $601 million in 1952, and then rose to $1.13 billion in 1956. United States Department of Commerce (unadjusted) statistics , 1/ which give a rough idea of free world trade with Communist China, indicate that it totaled $987 million in 1950, $638 million in 1952, $1.05 billion in 1956, and $1.47 billion in 1958. All available estimates agree, however, that Communist China's trade with the free world rose steadily during the first Five Year Plan period and, by 1958, reached a level which may have surpassed the value level (in current prices) of China's total trade with these same areas in the period just before the Communists came to power.

During recent years, Communist China has had a sizable export surplus in its trade with the free world. It has probably utilized this surplus to help make up its deficit in commodity trade with the Soviet bloc, and also to buy some goods indirectly from the West through Soviet bloc countries in order to circumvent Western trade restrictions. In the past several years this export surplus in direct trade with the free world has averaged between $100 million and $200 million each year.

Communist China's major imports from the free world since the start of its first Five Year Plan have been chemical fertilizers, crude rubber, cotton and wool, scientific instruments of various sorts, and miscellaneous dyestuffs and chemicals. According to U.S. Commerce Department figures, Chinese imports of fertilizers rose steadily, reaching roughly $60 million in 1956. With the exception of 1955, rubber imports have been running close to $50 million a year. Cotton imports have fluctuated considerably, between roughly $20 million and $60 million annually, but $40 million seems to have been about the average. Wool imports have risen steadily to over $30 million. General chemical imports have consistently been over $20 million a year. Imports of dyestuffs were at one point over $20 million, but recently appear to have been greatly reduced from that peak.

To pay for these and other imports from the free world, Communist China's most important exports to non-Communist countries during recent years have consisted of agricultural commodities including soya beans, grain, vegetable oils, fruits and vegetables, pork, dairy products, tea, and silk. U.S. Commerce Department figures indicate that China's soya beans exports to free world nations have been in the vicinity of $40 million a year, and that rice exports have averaged from $40 million to $50 million annually. Exports of fruits and vegetables have likewise been averaging roughly $40 million to $50 million annually. Pork and live pig exports have risen steadily from approximately $20 million to about $30 million, at least until the drop in 1957. A large percentage of total Chinese exports to the free world has consisted of smaller amounts of many traditional Chinese agricultural products and by-products. For example, anywhere from $10 million to $30 million of tea and between $5 million and $10 million of silk have been exported to free world countries each year, and Chinese exports to non-Communist countries of many items such as pig bristle, feathers, tung oil, and plant seeds have each averaged roughly $10 million to $15 million annually.

One of the most important recent developments in China's trade with the free world has been the rising level of cotton textile exports. These exports were under $5 million a year at the start of the first Five Year Plan period, but by the end of the Plan period they rose to a level which was probably between $20 million and $30 million, and there have been numerous indications during 1958 that they increased still more. Total exports of machinery and metals, although still relatively small, are also rising.

Exports of basic raw materials such as iron and coal, which Communist China hopes to increase substantially in the future, have been relatively small during the past few years, according to U. S. Commerce Department figures. Although exports of these items have been increasing, in most years during the first Five Year Plan period, Communist China's exports of iron ore to non-Communist countries were under $1 million annually, while coal exports to the free world were only between $10 million and $15 million even by 1956. U.S. Commerce Department figures on actual Chinese coal exports to major free world purchasers during 1956, indicate totals of 557,000 tons to Japan, 143,000 tons to Pakistan, and a little over 100,000 tons to Hong Kong (some for re-export). Recorded Chinese exports of iron ore to Japan in 1956 were only 11,000 tons. In 1957, Communist China, according to Japanese statistics, furnished only 483,000 tons of coal, 29,000 tons of pig iron, and 3,000 tons of iron ore to Japan.

Perhaps the most significant recent development in the direction of

Communist China's trade, in relation to free world areas, has been the substantial increase in the relative importance of countries in the Asian-African area compared with Europe and North America. By 1956, roughly two thirds of Communist China's total free world trade -- including about one half of its free world imports and about 70 percent of its free world exports -- were with countries in the Asian-African area. Peking has itself stressed the political significance of this trend.

It appears valid to make a distinction between Communist China's approach toward the major Western trading nations in Europe and its approach to Japan and the underdeveloped nations of the Asian-African region. The Chinese Communists' trade with Europe has had relatively few political implications. But Communist China's trade policies toward both Japan and the economically underdeveloped countries have had very strong political undertones -- in many instances, political motives seem to have been as important as economic aims.

Peking has concentrated major efforts upon developing its trade with countries in the Asian-African area. Often the Chinese Communists publish figures or percentages in reference to trade with the Asian-African area as a whole, and they now claim that during Communist China's first Plan period, trade with this area made up 16 percent of its total foreign trade. By comparison, trade with the West -- that is, mainly Europe -- was said to be only about 9 percent. U.S. Department of Commerce figures indicate that Peking's trade with all non-Communist countries in Asia, the Middle East, and Africa totaled $716 million in 1956, whereas its trade during that year with all OEEC countries (Western Europe minus Spain, but plus Turkey) was only $362 million.

There have been strong economic motives for development of this trade. Peking has had an urgent need to earn foreign exchange in these areas. But the Chinese Communists' political aims have been important as well. Specific political motives may have varied from country to country, but underlying all of China's trade with the Asian-African area is the assumption that growing trade will increase Communist China's prestige and influence and will pave the way for closer political relations. As one Chinese Communist publication put it in 1958, there should be "greater economic cooperation among Asian and African countries to free themselves quickly from the economic enslavement by imperialism and drive off the waves of the U.S. economic crisis."

In specific instances, Peking has helped certain countries in the Asian-African area to market their export surpluses. In other cases, it has set out to capture important markets for manufactured goods from Western countries, and from Japan and India. Consistently, it has used trade policies as a lever to promote closer political relations. And, in the case of Japan, it has attempted to use trade not only as a wedge in its efforts to obtain recognition and establish diplomatic relations but also as a crude weapon to influence domestic Japanese politics.

The largest free world trader with Communist China has been Hong Kong. This British colony obtains many of its own food and other requirements from the China mainland, and it is also a major entrepôt for Chinese Communist trade with other areas. The role of Hong Kong in China's trade is primarily that of an exchange earner, however, and Hong Kong-China trade has changed greatly in recent years. Hong Kong's exports to Communist China have steadily dropped, as Peking has expanded its direct trade relations with other areas, but Chinese Communist exports to Hong Kong have continued to increase. Because of Peking's large export surplus in its trade with Hong Kong, Communist China earns more foreign exchange there than in other free world areas.

In 1957, for example, Chinese Communist exports to Hong Kong were $198 million, while its imports from Hong Kong were $22 million -- in rough terms, about one third to one half of all Chinese Communist exports to Hong Kong are re-exported to other areas. One notable recent development in trade between the China mainland and Hong Kong has been the increase in exports of Chinese Communist manufactured goods, especially textiles. In 1957, Communist China exported close to $30 million of cotton yarn, fabrics, and clothing to Hong Kong, causing distress in the domestic industry of the area. China has also become Hong Kong's major source of supply for coal, cement, glass, and miscellaneous manufactured goods, as well as of traditional agricultural products.

Apart from Hong Kong, the most important free world trader with Communist China in recent years had been Japan. But the course of development of Sino-Japanese trade has been a turbulent one, and it provides the most striking example to date of Peking's inclination to think of trade in political terms. 2/ Following the 1952 "trade agreement" mentioned earlier, there was a tremendous amount of promotional activity in both Japan and Communist China, and Peking signed two more agreements with Japanese business groups in 1953 and 1955. The economic motivation for increased trade appeared to be fairly strong on both sides. It was particularly strong in Japan, but the Chinese Communists indicated that they would like to obtain more manufactured goods, especially capital goods, from the Japanese. On their part, the Japanese, remembering prewar days when 15 percent of Japan's total trade was with China, hoped to obtain increasing amounts of raw materials as well as agricultural goods from China and to find expanding markets there.

The actual growth of trade between Communist China and Japan was quite substantial through 1956, even though it fell considerably short of what some Japanese businessmen had hoped for. From a low of roughly $15 million in 1952, it rose to about $150 million in 1956, when the Chinese Communists imported about $84 million of goods from Japan and exported $67 million to Japan. The major Chinese exports to Japan were soya beans, rice, and salt; other exports were magnesia clinker, silk, tung oil, coal, and rosin. The Chinese bought a wide variety of manufactured products from the Japanese, including chemical fertilizers and insecticides, textile machinery, cement, synthetic and other textile yarns and fabrics, and miscellaneous chemicals, machines, and instruments. In 1957, however, due to economic difficulties in Communist China, the overall cutback in Communist China's foreign trade, and the failure to sign a new "trade agreement," Sino-Japanese trade dropped considerably to about $141 million. This figure represented no more than 2 percent of Japan's total trade.

Despite the difficulties in developing Sino-Japanese trade, many Japanese continued, at least through 1957, to indulge in wishful thinking about restoring trade with China. Some Japanese tended to disregard fundamental factors which have changed since the prewar period. Communist China is no longer importing large quantities of consumer goods which made up a sizable proportion of Japan's prewar exports to China. And the Peking regime has committed a large percentage of its own export capacity to the Soviet bloc, a fact which imposes limits on its ability to expand rapidly its trade with countries such as Japan. Many Japanese also underestimated the degree to which the Chinese Communists might be willing to subordinate economic interests to political considerations.

In the fall of 1957, when negotiations between Peking and Japanese businessmen for a fourth, nonofficial "trade agreement" began, the Chinese Communists started to press hard for political aims. Finally, the Japanese government, although not directly involved in the negotiations, was induced to make important concessions -- including an agreement to allow an exchange of permanent trade missions -- and a nonofficial trade pact was signed in early 1958 calling for shipments of roughly $100 million each way during 1958. At about the same time, representatives of the Japanese steel industry also signed an agreement with Peking calling for an exchange of Japanese steel products for Chinese coal and iron ore (plus, it was later indicated, rice), totaling close to $300 million each way over the five year period of 1958-62.

In May 1958, however, the Chinese Communists chose to press a purely political issue -- the refusal of the Japanese government to guarantee protection for the Chinese Communist flag -- and decided to bring strong economic pressure to bear upon Japan. Peking protested Tokyo's stand on the flag issue, denounced the Kishi government in very strong terms, and broke off all trade relations with Japan. This radical move was followed by numerous other measures of Chinese pressure against the Japanese, including a refusal to sign any new Sino-Japanese fishery agreement to replace the nonofficial agreement which expired in June. Peking's political propaganda at the time made it clear that the Chinese Communist decision to impose a total ban on trade with Japan was due not only to its hope that strong economic pressure might force the Japanese government to make additional political concessions, but also to the hope that a tough policy would help the Socialists defeat the Kishi government in the forthcoming Japanese elections. If anything, however, its action probably hurt the Socialists, and in any case Kishi won the election handily. Nationalist China, whose trade with Japan in 1957 was still somewhat larger than that of Communist China, also brought strong pressure to bear on Japan over the flag issue in an attempt to forestall Japanese concessions to Peking, and this pressure reinforced Japanese opinion which opposed giving in to Chinese Communist demands.

However, throughout 1958, the Chinese Communists continued to maintain their adament position, demanding an apology for the desecration of the Chinese Communist flag in Japan, and calling on the Japanese people to oppose Kishi, and this unrelenting pressure had some effect on the Japanese. The Kishi government decided in late 1958 that it would, after all, be willing to give certain guarantees concerning the Chinese Communists' right to fly their flag in Japan, but Peking was not satisfied and showed no immediate signs of softening its position.

Because of these events the immediate future of Sino-Japanese trade is uncertain. Peking's demonstration, during 1958, of its ability and willingness to manipulate trade for political purposes may have given many Japanese second thoughts about the desirability of becoming too dependent upon trade with Communist China. 3/ Nevertheless, in Japan, the pressure for developing all trade is such a fundamental element in national life that in time the Japanese may decide to make further concessions to Peking -- or, possibly, Peking might moderate its adament position. In the meantime, the Japanese are fearful of the ever-growing competition by Communist China in Southeast Asia, and so are the other exporters to this area.

In the long run, therefore, the possibility of a greater increase in Sino-Japanese trade, once resumed, cannot be ruled out. Under certain conditions, the Chinese Communists in all probability still would like to purchase more capital goods from Japan, and Peking could shift some of its purchases in this field from the Soviet bloc to the free world. In any large expansion of trade with Japan, Peking might encounter difficult payments problems, but it could make greater efforts to increase exports of Hainan iron and Kailan coal to Japan. Before World War II, Japan imported a large share of its coal from the Kailan mines, and the half million tons or so imported from China in 1956 amounted to only a fraction of the prewar level. In 1956, Japan imported over 6 million tons of iron ore from other parts of Asia, and only negligible amounts of this came from Communist China. The Japanese undoubtedly could use once again the million tons or so a year which they once obtained from Hainan.

There is little doubt that if trade relations are restored and if Sino-Japanese trade does increase substantially, this fact would have important political implications. If trade developed very far, there would be a definite possibility that Peking might develop more effective leverage than it now has to attempt to influence Japanese policies -- by threatening to cut off sources of supply or markets important to Japan. The effectiveness of such leverage would depend to a considerable degree, however, upon Japan's ability to turn to the West, and especially to the United States, for assistance in the event of pressure from Peking.

Southeast Asia is another area of growing importance in Communist China's foreign trade, and Peking's trade pattern with this area is different from China's trade relations with any other region. The Chinese Communists have begun to penetrate Southeast Asia markets for manufactured goods on a fairly large scale, and the bulk of Chinese consumer goods exports as well as some of its capital goods exports are going to this area. In return, Communist China is receiving agricultural products and raw materials from Southeast Asia. This exchange of manufactured goods for nonindustrial commodities is the reverse of the overall pattern characterizing Communist China's total foreign trade. Although there is a sound economic basis for much of the trade -- and recently the desire to step up exchange earnings in this region appears to have become increasingly important to Peking -- the Chinese Communists have frankly stated their belief that the development of trade relations with Southeast Asia is designed to promote closer political relations and increased Communist influence in that area.

The Chinese Communists claim that their trade with Southeast Asia rose 15 percent in 1955, and 40 percent in 1956. U. S. Government statistics indicate that between 1954 and 1957, Communist China's trade with the underdeveloped non-Communist nations in the Far East and Southeast

Asia increased by over three quarters, at a rate three times as fast as the increase in Japan's trade with the region, though in absolute terms, Japan's trade with the area of $2.3 billion in 1957 was nearly four times that of China. During 1958, there has been clear evidence of a major Chinese Communist export drive in Southeast Asia. Although the exact dimensions of this effort will not be wholly clear until final trade statistics for the year become available, it has already cut into the markets for many products, including textiles, which Japan and India have developed in that region in the past.

Peking has recently resorted to price cutting in order to capture Southeast Asian markets for manufactured goods. In 1958, it adopted a policy of selling textiles and many other products at prices 5 to 10 percent below the prices for comparable Japanese and Indian goods. It has pressed overseas Chinese businessmen in the region to foster the sale of Chinese goods, and in some instances it has advised them specifically to boycott Japanese products. Whether this export drive is primarily a response to the rupture of Sino-Japanese trade, an effort to earn foreign exchange, or a campaign to extend Peking's economic and political influence by dumping, is not yet clear, but it has already caused considerable alarm in Japan.

Communist China's first important trade agreement with a Southeast Asian country was with Ceylon, and Peking's trade relations with Ceylon are extremely significant in both economic and political terms. The 1952 rice-rubber barter agreement between the two countries was a case in which Communist China stepped in and simultaneously helped to solve a small nation's problem of marketing a major export product, helped to undermine the restrictions on trade with China (rubber was an embargoed item), complicated the relations of that country with the United States, and assured itself access to much-needed supplies of rubber. In 1952, Ceylon was having difficulties marketing its rubber at prices which it hoped to obtain. Communist China in this situation offered to buy at prices above those prevailing on the world market.

The five year agreement, valid for the period 1953-57, called for an annual exchange of 50,000 tons of rubber for 270,000 tons of rice. When this agreement ended in 1957, a new one year agreement was signed calling for a minimum trade of roughly $20 million each way, with Ceylon providing rubber plus some other commodities, and China sending 200,000 tons of rice and various other goods such as steel and coal. The price Peking agreed to pay for rubber this time was lower than previously, but the Chinese Communists helped to compensate for this by announcing an economic aid program to Ceylon at the same time (to be discussed in Chapter Ten).

Peking's trade relations with Burma have followed a similar pattern, although on a smaller scale. In April 1954, a three year trade agreement was signed, and a protocol later in the same year called for the exchange of Burmese rice for Chinese goods, at a time when Burma was having difficulty in marketing rice, which is its main export commodity. In December 1955, another protocol specified that Communist China would buy 150,000 tons of rice from Burma, and late in 1956 Peking claimed that this amount had been purchased in each of the previous two years. Communist China's rice situation and trade dealings in this period presented a fairly odd picture. Although experiencing domestic shortages, the Chinese

Communists were exporting altogether about a million tons of rice a year, and part of their purchases of Burmese rice was re-exported.

Apart from rice, they also bought some cotton and rubber from Burma. In return, the major Chinese exports to Burma have included cotton yarn and cloth, other textiles such as silk and knitted goods, building materials, and machinery. Overall Sino-Burmese trade rose from under $1 million in 1954 to over $30 million in 1956, and then dropped somewhat in the following year. In July 1956, a contract was signed for China to provide complete equipment to expand a textile mill in Burma by over 20,000 spindles and close to 200 looms, and Chinese experts went along to help construct the mill and install the machinery. In late 1957, Peking agreed to help build a new mill with 40,000 spindles in Burma. And in early 1958, Burma and China signed a new trade agreement on a one year basis.

Sino-Indonesian trade has risen steadily since the first trade agreement between the two countries was signed in late 1953, and the supplementing protocol and payments agreement were concluded in the following year. In 1956, a second trade agreement was signed calling for the exchange of £12 million ($34 million) of goods in each direction. Under these agreements, Communist China's trade with Indonesia rose from $2 million in 1953 to $53 million in 1957. Peking's exports to Indonesia have consisted to a very large extent of manufactured goods. Cotton textiles have been by far the most important single item, but included also have been a wide variety of consumer goods and some machines and appliances. Indonesia had difficulty in 1956 in meeting its export commitments to Communist China, however, and the Chinese decided to give the Indonesians three more years, or until 1959, to settle their trade deficit under the 1954 protocol; but this difficulty became less important when rubber exports to China rose in 1957. Copra and sugar constituted the principal Indonesian exports to the Chinese until 1957 -- although such items as pepper, rattan, hemp, and citronella oil were important too -- but rubber is now a major item.

Communist China has also developed its trade with other South and Southeast Asian countries. Trade with Pakistan has consisted largely of an exchange of Chinese coal, plus some rice, iron, newsprint, and silk, for Pakistan's cotton. In return for about 200,000 tons of cotton obtained from Pakistan in the seven years up to 1957, Communist China shipped several hundred thousand tons of coal, and in two contracts signed during 1956, the Chinese Communists agreed to sell Pakistan 325,000 tons of coal. In 1958, Peking signed another large coal-for-cotton barter deal with Pakistan. Sino-Indian trade, since the first general intergovernmental trade agreement in 1954, has consisted largely of an exchange of Chinese silk, rice, newsprint, chemicals, and manufactured goods for Indian cotton, tobacco, gunny bags, and pepper. In early 1956, Communist China and Cambodia signed a £ 5 million ($14 million) trade agreement under which Peking is supplying textile machinery, small capital goods of several sorts, steel, building materials, raw materials, and food in exchange for such varied Cambodian products as rubber, corn, tobacco, and timber.

In recent years, Singapore - Malaya has been the leading Southeast-Asian trader with China. From 1953 through 1956, this trade was largely one-way, since rubber exports to Communist China were barred by the British. Peking supplied goods desired by the large overseas Chinese population in that area, and Singapore-Malaya was Communist China's second largest area of net foreign exchange earnings, after Hong Kong. In 1956, for example, of a total two-way Sino-Malayan trade of over $50 million, Peking exported $43 million and imported $8 million. This has changed, however, as a result of the renewal of the rubber trade. Two-way trade jumped to $76 million in 1957, as Peking pushed sales of textiles and other manufactured goods and bought rubber, and of this total Singapore-Malaya's exports had risen to $24 million. In 1958 trade rose further, but Peking's export drive caused Singapore-Malaya such concern that the authorities there imposed restrictions on Chinese textiles and on Peking's banking activities. The Thai government also imposed severe restrictions on Chinese imports in late 1958.

One further development in Communist China's trade with non-Communist countries deserves mention. Paralleling the Chinese Communist efforts to develop closer diplomatic relations with key Middle Eastern countries, especially Egypt and Syria, there has been a conscious effort by Peking to foster Communist China's trade in this area. In the case of Egypt in particular, trade development has been significant since the 1955 trade pact and accompanying protocol calling for Egyptian £ 10 million ($28 million) trade each way, and Egypt is now one of Peking's largest trading partners. In 1956, another protocol raised the level to Egyptian £ 12 million ($34 million), and the 1957 protocol raised it still further to £ 13 million ($36 million). In 1956-57, an even larger rise in Sino-Egyptian trade took place, from $35 million in 1956 to $63 million in 1957. In this exchange the Chinese Communists' principal imports from Egypt have been raw cotton and cotton yarn; their major exports have included steel products, machinery, vegetable oils, and fats.

Peking also trades on a significant level with Morocco, although to date this trade is almost entirely one-sided, consisting of Chinese tea exports to the Moroccans. Communist China's desire to promote trade with other African and Middle Eastern countries is indicated by the fact that Peking signed trade agreements with Syria and Lebanon in 1955, sent trade delegations or missions to Saudi Arabia, Ethiopia, and the Sudan in 1956, signed a five year trade agreement with Yemen in early 1958, and concluded trade agreements with Tunisia, Morocco, and Iraq in late 1958 or early 1959.

Although Communist China's total trade with Europe is considerably less than its total trade with Asian nations, it too has increased significantly during the past few years, and particularly since 1955. West Germany is now the largest European trader with Communist China, followed by Great Britain -- their trade with Communist China in 1958 was $221 million and $128 million respectively. In 1958, West Germany's trade with Communist China was greater than that of any non-Communist Asian area except Hong Kong, while Britain's trade with China was somewhat above that of Malaya.

Communist China's trade level with each of several other European countries including France, Switzerland, Belgium, Italy, and the Netherlands ranges from roughly $20 million up to $40 million annually. Peking's trade with these European countries, however, follows more closely the traditional Chinese pattern of foreign trade, with China's agricultural products being exchanged for Western manufactured goods plus some industrial raw materials. Chemical fertilizers, other chemicals, dyestuffs, machines, equipment, instruments, watches, wool, medicines, some tractors and other vehicles, synthetic yarns, and metals are among the important exports from European countries to China, and Peking has been exporting to them traditional Chinese animal and vegetable products for the most part. In recent years, the Chinese Communists have had a slight export surplus with Europe, in contrast to a very large one with Asian countries, but currently the balance seems to be swinging the other way, and the Chinese are now importing more than they export in trade with Europe.

Of all the recent developments in Communist China's trade with free world areas, the most notable have been the growing exports of manufactured goods and the Chinese Communists' recent expansion of trade with the Asian-African countries. The latter trend is clearly related to a general drive on the part of the whole Communist bloc to promote trade and increase the bloc's economic as well as political influence in the underdeveloped regions of the world. At present, Communist China accounts for roughly one fifth of the Communist bloc's total trade with the whole free world, but Peking's trade with Southeast Asia, South Asia, and the Far East accounted for approximately four fifths of total Communist bloc trade with these areas by 1956.

Communist China's trade policies in Southeast Asia give the greatest cause for concern to the West. Even though it is not yet completely clear whether the Chinese Communists are embarking upon a policy of deliberate dumping for political purposes, Peking's trade policies could have a very disruptive effect upon Southeast Asia and an adverse economic impact upon both Japan and India. To date, despite the rapid recent growth of Communist Chinese trade in Southeast Asia, Peking still plays only a minor role in the total trade of the region. In 1958, for example, trade with Communist China represented only 5 percent of Ceylon's trade, 3 percent of Burma's, 2 percent of Indonesia's and 4 percent of Singapore-Malaya's, and even less in the case of other Southeast Asian countries. But as Peking's trade grows, as it seems destined to do, the West might have to consider action to counterbalance unfair trade practices used by the Chinese Communists, to counteract possible disruption in Southeast Asia caused by trade manipulation, or to give further assistance to Japan and India if the loss of trade in Southeast Asia complicates their economic problems.

Chapter Ten

FOREIGN AID AND BALANCE OF PAYMENTS

One of the most remarkable developments in Communist China's economic policies during the first Five Year Plan period was Peking's decision to embark upon foreign aid programs of its own. It is a surprising fact that since 1956 the Chinese Communists, despite their great needs and problems domestically, have been giving much more financial assistance than they have been receiving. From the time Peking's first foreign aid program was started in 1953, and until 1956, all of Communist China's foreign aid was granted to neighboring Communist states. But since 1956, the Chinese Communists have extended economic assistance to a number of free world countries, and have assumed a place in this aspect of economic competition with the West as well as in the current trade competition between the Communist and non-Communist worlds.

The total amount of Communist China's foreign assistance during the first Five Year Plan period was substantial. It probably totaled about $647 million, although part of this may have been merely a write-off of Chinese costs incurred in assisting the North Korean regime during the Korean conflict. Specific figures are lacking for Chinese foreign aid during 1953-54, but it can be estimated that it probably totaled approximately $118 million during those two years. Available data on Peking's budgets for later years include concrete statistics on Communist China's foreign aid, which amounted to $166 million in 1955, $171 million in 1956, and $192 million in 1957 (see Appendix Table 7).

The total amount of publicly-announced Chinese grants of economic aid, about which some details are known, was $779 million during 1953-57, but delivery on many of these grants has continued since 1957. Of this $779 million, an overwhelming majority, amounting to $724 million was granted by Peking to other Communist countries (North Korea, North Vietnam, Outer Mongolia, and Hungary), but $55 million consisted of Chinese Communist grants to non-Communist countries in the Asian-African area (Cambodia, Nepal, Ceylon, and Egypt).

A further remarkable fact is that all of the above-mentioned economic aid consisted of grants rather than credits or loans, a fact which is doubly striking since Soviet financial assistance to Peking has been on a loan rather than on a grant basis. In addition to this grant aid, furthermore, Peking during the first Five Year Plan period gave one long-term loan of $25 million to Hungary, and during late 1957 and early 1958 it offered long-term loans to Burma, Yemen, Indonesia, and Ceylon.

Communist China's ventures into the foreign aid field began in November 1953, with a grant of roughly $338 million to North Korea, to be used over the four year period of 1954-57, for economic rehabilitation after the Korean War. A similar grant, also of approximately $338 million, was made by Peking in July 1955, to North Vietnam; this, too, was for postwar rehabilitation, and was to be used during the period 1955-59. In August 1956, Communist China gave a grant to Outer Mongolia of $40 million to help in industrial and other economic development projects there during the 1956-59 period. When the Hungarian revolt took place, Peking, in November 1956, extended a $7.5 million grant to the Kadar government. Other Chinese Communist assistance to nations within the Soviet bloc during the 1953-57 period included a long-term credit to Albania in December 1954, about which no details are known, and the above-mentioned $25 million long-term credit to Hungary in May 1957 -- the latter carries an interest rate of 2 percent, and is to be repaid in ten years from 1960.

Since the start of Communist China's second Five Year Plan, Peking has announced substantial additional aid, in the form of both grants and loans, to its Asian Communist neighbors. In September 1958, two separate loans to North Korea were announced. One was to help the Koreans pay their share of the costs of a joint Sino-Korean power plant project on the Yalu River; while the other was for the construction of several industrial plants in North Korea. The size of these loans was not made public, however. In December 1958, Peking publicized a long-term loan to Outer Mongolia, totaling $25 million, for the construction of various factories and power plants. Delivery of this loan is to take place through 1961, and repayment is to be made in 15 years, starting in 1962. In February 1959, the Chinese Communists announced a new grant plus a loan to North Vietnam, to be used for the construction of 49 industrial and communications enterprises. The grant amounted to roughly $42 million. The loan, amounting to about $169 million, is to be repaid, with 1 percent interest, during a ten year period starting in 1967.

Communist China has been supplying to all of these recipients of its aid sizable quantities of manufactured consumer goods and capital goods as well as industrial raw materials, including many specific items which the Chinese themselves must import. Peking's aid deliveries to North Korea have included locomotives, freight and passenger cars, communications equipment, machinery, agricultural implements, metal products, electric motors, textile machinery, chemical raw materials, building materials, cement, coal, steel, cotton fabrics, paper, miscellaneous consumer goods, and grain. Similar types of equipment and commodities have been sent to North Vietnam, including specifically the materials needed to restore or construct textile mills, leather tanneries, electrical equipment factories, agricultural implement plants, paper mills, factories to produce medical equipment, petroleum installations, railway lines, conservation works, and meteorological stations. In Outer Mongolia, the Chinese Communists are helping to build a textile plant, brick kiln, plywood factory, glass works, and numerous other installations including a stadium, gymnasium, and housing.

Technical assistance has also been an important part of Peking's aid program to North Korea, North Vietnam, and Outer Mongolia. The Chinese army railway corps has helped to restore transport in North Korea and North Vietnam, and Peking has not only sent a large number of Chinese civilian technicians to North Korea, North Vietnam, and Outer Mongolia, but has also received a significant number of workers and technicians from these areas and has provided them with training in Communist China.

A fairly large flow of Chinese workers has gone to Outer Mongolia; over 10,000 are reported to have gone in the one year period preceding August 1956, alone.

Communist China's economic aid programs to its Communist neighbors have without doubt reinforced or increased Peking's influence in these areas. It is interesting to note that Peking's economic aid to North Korea and North Vietnam has exceeded that of the Soviet Union, and the flow of Chinese workers to Outer Mongolia is a development which may have considerable long-range significance. Beyond this, however, these aid programs are suggestive of Peking's potential capabilities for extending economic aid to countries outside of the Communist bloc on a larger scale than heretofore if Communist China's leaders decide to do so.

In comparison with its economic aid to Asian Communist countries, Peking's programs of economic assistance to free world countries have been relatively small to date, but they have been of considerable local importance nonetheless. Communist China's economic grants to Cambodia, Nepal, and Ceylon have been designed to reinforce Peking's general policy of encouraging neutralism in South and Southeast Asia and fostering closer Chinese relations and greater Chinese influence in these areas. Its loan offers to Burma and Indonesia, as well as Ceylon, presumably have had the same aim. The economic grant by Peking to Egypt and its loan to Yemen reflect the steady increase of Chinese Communist interest and influence in the Middle East. To date, Peking's economic aid to these areas is still considerably smaller than assistance to these areas from either the major Western countries or from the Soviet Union, but it has been large enough to constitute a factor of real importance in some of the smaller countries which have received the aid, and its significance in overall economic competition between the Communist bloc and the West should not be underestimated.

Communist China's first economic aid program to a non-Communist country was started in mid-1956. In June 1956, the Chinese Communists signed an agreement with the Cambodians under which China gave Cambodia a grant of $22.4 million to be delivered over a period of two to three years. The Chinese promised to send the necessary equipment and technicians to build four factories in Cambodia -- a textile plant, cement plant, paper mill, and plywood factory -- and in November 1956 the first group of Chinese technicians arrived in Pnom Penh to begin the work of surveying and designing. Chinese aid to Cambodia also is to include various types of commodities and supplies. The first inventory of desired goods, drawn up by the Cambodians in December 1956, included items valued at $5.6 million, among which were textiles, round iron bars, cement, paper, pottery, and porcelain. The government of Cambodia stated it would sell these supplies through businessmen. Actual deliveries began in mid-1957 when the first installment of roughly $1.4 million was announced; the Cambodian government revealed that half of this would be used for developing agriculture and irrigation and the other half for social welfare.

It appears, therefore, that part of the Chinese aid to Cambodia will be sent in the form of commodities which the Cambodian government can sell to help various of its own programs, while part will be devoted to the building of four factories with the help of Chinese technicians. Chinese technical assistance is likely to be somewhat less important, however, than in the Korean, Vietnamese, and Mongolian aid programs. In 1958, when Cambodia and Communist China established formal diplomatic relations, the Chinese Communists offered additional free aid, including a small iron and steel mill.

In the fall of 1956, Peking announced another small aid program, this time to Nepal for use in the five year economic plan. In October, an agreement was signed in Peking whereby the Chinese Communists agreed to grant Nepal, over a three year period, roughly $12.6 million, one third of which would be in foreign exchange, and two thirds in commodities, equipment, and supplies to be determined by negotiations. As in the case of Peking's other aid agreements, great stress was placed upon the assertion that "no conditions whatsoever" were attached to the assistance and that no repayment was required. One unique feature of the Nepal aid agreement was the specific stipulation that no Chinese technical personnel would be sent along with the aid to Nepal, an indication of Nepalese sensitivity about maintaining neutralism and suspicion about the possible political implications of accepting Chinese technicians. Very little information is available on deliveries of the $8.4 million of supplies and equipment involved in the aid program, but one half of the $4.2 million of foreign exchange promised was reportedly turned over to Nepal in February 1957, and the remaining half was promised for 1958.

In November 1956, the crisis in Egypt brought forth another grant of Chinese Communist economic aid. When the Anglo-French invasion of Suez took place, Peking announced a grant of roughly $4.7 million in cash to Egypt, and at the same time it speeded up shipments of commodities under a recently concluded Sino-Egyptian trade agreement. This was really an emergency assistance program given as concrete evidence of Communist China's political support for the Egyptians.

In September 1957, the Chinese Communists gave a grant to Ceylon of approximately $15.75 million. Under an agreement signed with Ceylon in September 1957, Peking agreed to give this amount to Ceylon with "no strings attached," to be used over the five year period 1958-62, particularly for improvement of rubber plantations. This program fitted very well into the pattern established by the Cambodian and Nepalese agreements. Once again the recipient was a small, neutralist-inclined country. In addition, however, a special situation led to Communist China's decision to make a grant to Ceylon at that particular time, when it also signed a new rice-for-rubber barter pact with Ceylon. At the expiration of the five year barter agreement which had governed China-Ceylon trade up until 1957, the Chinese insisted upon setting a lower price for Ceylonese rubber in a new agreement. The grant of aid was, in a sense, partial compensation to Ceylon for the lower price which China will pay for rubber in the future.

In its trade relations with Southeast Asia, Communist China has also shown itself willing to give short-term trading credit in special circumstances. This is, in effect, what the Chinese did in 1956 in their trade with Indonesia. Because the Indonesians were lagging in fulfillment of their export obligations to China under the 1954 Sino-Indonesia trade protocol, the Chinese agreed to let Indonesia postpone fulfilling these obligations, giving it three years, 1957-59, to make up past deficits.

Since late 1957, the Chinese Communists have added a new element in their foreign aid activities by offering long-term loans to several non-Communist countries in the Asian-African area. The largest of these have been to Indonesia. In early 1958, an Indonesian official revealed that Peking had offered Indonesia long-term credits, some of the proceeds of which could be used for industrial development purposes. Later in 1958, it was reported specifically that the Chinese had provided Indonesia long-term loans for the purchase of consumer goods, including 75 million yards of textiles and 25,000 tons of rice. These credits, totaling roughly $11.2 million, must be repaid by Indonesia in ten years and bear 2.5 percent interest. Still more recent reports indicate that Indonesia is considering the acceptance of another $40 million, possibly including the cost of a textile factory and a steel mill.

In early 1958, a Burmese Deputy Premier, returning home from Communist China, announced that the Chinese had offered Burma a loan amounting to the equivalent of roughly $4 million, at 2.5 percent interest, for expansion of the Burmese textile industry. In January 1958, it was announced in Peking that an agreement had been signed with Yemen involving a long-term loan amounting to about $16.38 million to be used for construction of a motor road, a textile mill, a cigarette factory, and other plants. This agreement stipulated that Chinese technicians and workers will be sent to Yemen to work on these projects. In March 1958, the Chinese Communists offered Ceylon a loan equal to roughly $10.5 million, for machinery and equipment to be used for the rehabilitation of flood-damaged areas. In September, Ceylon accepted the loan on terms which called for delivery of the credit in four annual installments, 2.5 percent interest charges, and repayment in ten years starting in 1961. During 1958, Peking also made an informal offer to build a small iron and steel mill in Indonesia and expressed China's willingness "to give further assistance within its ability" to Indonesia.

Although numerous Koreans, Vietnamese, and Mongols have been given technical training by the Chinese Communists in China's educational institutions and factories, there is no indication that this type of technical assistance has been extended on any significant scale by Communist China to non-Communist countries to date. In 1956-57, over 500 foreign students from 23 countries were reported to be studying in institutions of higher learning in Communist China, but probably very few of these were from non-Communist countries. This figure does not include the very large number of overseas Chinese from Southeast Asia studying in Communist China. The number could well grow in the future, however, since there is very little doubt about Peking's willingness to accept them.

In many respects it is surprising that Communist China has been able to engage in foreign aid activities at all, in view not only of the major economic difficulties within China but also of the increasingly difficult overall balance of payments problem which Peking has encountered.

During the first Five Year Plan period, Communist China's major receipts in its overall balance of payments can be estimated, in rough terms, to have consisted of $9.92 billion from exports, $1.32 billion from Soviet loans and credits of all sorts, and about $804 million from miscellaneous receipts including overseas Chinese remittances and expenditures of foreigners in China. It can be estimated that during this same period, Peking's major outpayments went for roughly $10.6 billion in imports, $763 million in servicing and repayment of Soviet loans and credits, and $647 million in foreign aid from Communist China to other countries. In short, the total of Communist China's own foreign aid, plus its servicing and repayment of Soviet loans and credits, appears to have exceeded receipts during this period of all types of Soviet financial assistance. By the end of the first Five Year Plan period, the net outflow in these categories was very large. In 1957, when China received only $10 million in foreign aid from the Soviet Union, Peking paid out $192 million in its own aid programs and an estimated $274 million in servicing and repayment of past Soviet loans and credits.

The fact that Peking has been steadily increasing its foreign aid program during recent years, despite all of its domestic problems and balance of payment difficulties, is convincing testimony to the fact that Chinese Communist leaders regard foreign economic aid as an important instrument of their foreign policy. Already Communist China must maintain a sizable export surplus in its balance of payments, and to increase or even to continue the present level of China's foreign aid programs, Peking will have to expand its export surplus still further, adding to the burdens imposed upon China's domestic economy and increasing the economic sacrifices demanded of the Chinese people -- unless the Soviet Union decides to raise the level of its economic aid to Communist China. The Chinese Communists appear definitely to have established themselves in the foreign aid field, however, and Peking's grants, loans, and technical assistance to countries in the Asian-African area consititute a factor of rising importance in economic competition between the Communist bloc and the West.

CONCLUSION

The record of the 1953-57 period clearly indicates that Communist China has already become an important participant in the economic competition between the Communist bloc and the West, particularly as it affects the underdeveloped areas of Asia and Africa, and it is likely to continue to play a significant role in this competition. Peking faces numerous economic problems, and its balance of payments and other difficulties may well impose limitations upon its ability to participate in this contest to the degree which Peking's leaders undoubtedly would like. On the other hand, if its recent, claimed economic achievements are even close to the truth, Peking's capacity to expand trade and aid may rapidly increase.

The rate of economic growth and industrial expansion in Communist China during its first Five Year Plan period was very impressive. The Chinese claims that they increased national income by over 50 percent, gross national output by over 60 percent, gross industrial output by almost 120 percent, and gross agricultural output by roughly 25 percent, indicate a rapid process of development. The most notable gains were made in building up key heavy industries, such as iron, steel, and machine-building. As stated earlier, the official claims on achievements to date almost certainly exaggerate the rate of progress somewhat, but there cannot be any doubt about the fact that during the first Plan period the Chinese Communists initiated a development process of great importance, and apparently the pace of development in China has actually speeded up since 1958. Clearly Communist China is now probably making more rapid progress in building industrial power than any other major underdeveloped nation, even allowing for population growth, and it would be a serious mistake to underestimate the potential psychological and political impact of this fact in a period when the desire for modernization and economic progress is one of the strongest and most universal motivating forces in the underdeveloped areas of the world.

The price which the Chinese people have paid for the Peking regime's economic gains has been high, and since the start of the communization drive it appears that this price may be even higher in the future. Peking's policies have involved oppressive and often cruel totalitarian rule, purges and suppression of individual freedom, and revolutionary upheaval of Chinese society, as well as enforced austerity and economic hardship. The average of $3 to $4 billion per year which the Chinese Communists devoted to investment in new development projects during the first Plan period constituted a very heavy burden on the Chinese people and imposed constant strain on the Chinese economy. Furthermore, since most of the investment went into heavy industries, it contributed primarily to the growth of Communist China's industrial power rather than to improvement of the welfare of the population. It is difficult to predict, however, whether all the leaders of other underdeveloped areas can be counted upon to take the full social cost into consideration when they view the indisputable evidence of industrial expansion which Communist China has achieved.

There is no doubt that Peking's first Five Year Plan has put Communist China into the forefront of underdeveloped nations in terms of their rates of overall growth. If the annual increase in GNP during the first

Plan period was perhaps close to 7 or 8 percent, as recent studies indicate, the rate of growth in China has probably been close to double that of India -- where the government has struggled to carry out an economic development program stressing economic welfare within the framework of democratic institutions and individual freedom. If, over the years ahead the major non-Communist countries in the underdeveloped areas of the world are not able to achieve economic growth at a reasonably rapid pace, and if Peking forges ahead, this could be an extremely disturbing factor in the competitive struggle between the Communist bloc and the West. Conceivably, it could lead an increasing number of leaders in underdeveloped nations to think about using totalitarian methods of economic development despite the sacrifice of political freedom and individual welfare involved.

The economic development program in Communist China has already begun to change the traditional, agrarian character of Chinese society. The share of industry in China's national output rose from 21 percent in 1952 to 32 percent in 1956, and it has increased still more since 1956. It would, of course, take decades of growth at present rates for the Chinese Communist regime to approach the level of industrial achievement of the two largest industrial powers in the world. But there is definitely a possibility that in certain key heavy industries, which are of fundamental importance to modern military strength, Peking may in a relatively few years be able to catch up with or surpass Japan (in total output, not in per capita output), which is the only important industrial power in Asia at the present time.

In broad terms, Japan has achieved a level of industrialization which is vastly ahead of all other Asian nations, including China, 1/ but by concentrating their efforts on industries such as iron and steel and machine-building, the Chinese Communists may be able to catch up fairly rapidly with the Japanese in terms of output in these key industrial categories. For example, if Peking's present plans for increasing steel production can be implemented, Communist China will soon surpass Japan as a steel producer. The Chinese goal for 1959 is 18 million tons of steel. Japanese economists project a production total of about 20 million tons for 1962. 2/ If this happens, it could have a very great psychological, political, and military impact on Asia, particularly in view of the fact that a totalitarian regime can concentrate its use of available steel upon military and other uses directly related to national power.

In its foreign economic relations, the Peking regime has already given clear evidence of its desire to employ trade and foreign aid as instruments supporting its overall foreign policies and as weapons in the economic competition with the West. Even though the fundamental orientation of the Chinese economy is now toward the Soviet Union and other bloc countries -- in great contrast to the situation prior to Communist takeover in China -- Peking's economic relations with non-Communist countries have also developed substantially during the period of its first Five Year Plan, and they may continue to do so in the future.

During the first Plan period, Peking's dependence upon the Soviet bloc for technical assistance and for equipment and supplies essential to its industrialization program was very great, but contrary to a widely held assumption, the financial assistance to Communist China from the

Soviet Union has been limited, and the Chinese Communists have largely carried the financial burden of economic development themselves. It is undoubtedly fair to say that the Chinese Communists could not have implemented their first Five Year Plan without Soviet technical assistance, which has been of extraordinary importance in crucial sectors of the Chinese economy. Furthermore, of Communist China's total foreign trade, which rose from $2.7 billion in 1952 to $4.3 billion in 1957, close to four fifths was with the USSR and other bloc countries during the first Plan, and imports from the Soviet Bloc provided the most important capital goods required for industrial construction in China.

However, the Russians did not give Peking any financial grants during China's first Five Year Plan period. And of the claimed total of $1.31 billion of Soviet credits and loans of all kinds to Communist China during the first Plan, only a small part is definitely known to have consisted of long-term loans for economic development. By the end of 1957, furthermore, Peking had used up all past Soviet loans and credits, was paying the Russians large amounts (between $250 and $300 million annually) in servicing and repayment of past Soviet loans and credits, and thus had to support increasingly large export surpluses in its trade with the USSR.

Although it seems likely that there will be continued close integration of China's economy with the Soviet bloc, and continued Chinese Communist dependence upon the USSR and Satellites both for technical assistance and for capital goods required for Peking's industrialization program, Communist China's development program has not constituted a very heavy drain on the Soviet Union. The financial drain has been relatively small, and although there is evidence that the burden of supplying capital goods to Communist China has created problems for some of the European Satellites, it has not constituted an excessively burdensome load on the Soviet economy. It could be argued, in fact, that Communist China's contribution to the Communist bloc, not only in political and military terms but also in its role in overall Communist bloc economic policies toward the non-Communist world, may well have outweighed the economic contributions which the bloc has made to China. It is very possible that economic issues have been much more of a problem in Sino-Soviet relations than has been apparent, and they may continue to present difficulties in the future.

Since about 1952, when the Chinese Communists began actively promoting trade with the free world, Peking has concluded many important trade agreements with non-Communist nations, particularly with countries in the Asian-African area, and its trade with free world areas has risen to a level of approximately $1 billion annually. Roughly two thirds of this --including about one half of Communist China's imports and approximately 70 percent of its exports -- is with the Asian-African area, and Communist China now accounts for roughly four fifths of the entire Communist bloc's trade with the Far East and South and Southeast Asia. In their purchasing policies, the Chinese Communists have moved into situations where Asian countries were having difficulty marketing major export products and have become important buyers of these products. They have energetically invaded Asian markets for manufactured consumer goods and have also begun exporting some capital goods. And they have consistently attempted to use trade policies to foster closer political relations.

Peking's trade relations with Japan have provided a clear example of the Chinese Communists' willingness and ability to use trade as a weapon for political purposes -- even though to date Communist China has not yet been successful in achieving its aims in regard to Japan. The growth of Communist China's trade with Southeast Asia has great potential significance in both economic and political terms. In contrast to its trade pattern with most other areas, Peking has been exporting manufactured goods in sizable quantities, and importing agricultural commodities and raw materials in its trade with Southeast Asia. Already, the rising level of Chinese exports of textiles and other consumer goods constitutes serious competition with Japan and India in the markets of some Southeast Asian nations. And the fact that Peking has also begun exporting capital goods on a small scale has impressed many people in Southeast Asia, reinforcing Communist China's prestige and influence in the area.

Since 1956, the Chinese Communists have also entered the field of foreign aid to underdeveloped nations in the non-Communist world. The grants and loans offered by Communist China to non-Communist Asian nations since 1956 represent a new and important element in Peking's foreign economic policies. To date, this aid has not been very large if compared with that of either the United States or the USSR, but it has gone entirely to small neutralist-inclined countries in the Asian-African area -- countries which the Communist bloc views as very important areas of competition with the West -- and it has certainly reinforced Peking's overall policies toward these areas.

All of these developments and trends represent policies which Peking seems committed to pursue in the future. Whether or not it can do so effectively will depend to a considerable degree upon the course of economic development within China. The Chinese Communists face many problems. But they are also experimenting with some revolutionary solutions.

The most pressing economic problem which the Chinese Communists have encountered to date has been the lag in agricultural development. Agricultural output fell short of Peking's aims during the first Plan period, and this fact affected all segments of the Chinese economy. However, Communist China's dramatic irrigation and communization programs in 1958 may enable the Chinese Communists to make greater agricultural progress in the future. Peking claims, in fact, to have made spectacular progress already. But its recent claims still must be viewed with caution, and factors such as the peasants' reaction to communization are still unpredictable.

The explosive growth of population in China is another basic problem of tremendous proportions. With the population now increasing at roughly 12 or 13 million people a year, the Chinese Communists face a "Malthusian counterrevolution." To date, little progress has been made in solving this problem, and it is not apparent that Peking is even trying to face up to it at present. Since late 1957, in fact, the Chinese Communists have talked as if they feel confident that a growing population will actually mean faster economic progress, at least over the short term.

Since 1956, Communist China has also encountered increasing balance of payments problems. The absence of further Soviet loans and credits has required the Chinese Communists to increase exports steadily just to maintain past levels of foreign trade, but the pressures on the domestic economy have made it difficult to raise exports. In 1957, as a matter of fact, the level of exports and the volume of total foreign trade, had to be reduced below the level of the preceding year. In 1958, however, Communist China's exports and its total trade, rose once again, and Peking's claims about its "great leap forward" in 1958 raise the possibility that China may now be acquiring a broader domestic production base for increased exports -- if the Chinese Communists' recent claims are even partially true. As of early 1959, however, it seems necessary to reserve judgment on the actual magnitude of the Chinese Communists' achievements in 1958.

The future development of Communist China's economic relations with free world areas will, in any case, depend in large degree upon political decisions made by Peking's leaders. There is little doubt that a regime with the totalitarian power which the Chinese Communists possess will probably be able to increase exports and foreign aid, at least to some degree, if it decides it is important enough to do so, even though it may aggravate domestic economic problems.

The Chinese Communists might well decide to shift part of their present Soviet bloc trade to free world areas, and if they did this, their capacity to compete with the West economically might be significantly increased even without an increase in the total volume of their foreign trade. Although at present there is every reason to expect that Peking will maintain its primary economic orientation toward the Soviet bloc, the fact that since 1956 its trade with the free world has increased as a proportion of its total trade is significant. At the moment there is still no sign that the existing impasse in Sino-Japanese relations will soon be broken, but if trade between Communist China and Japan were to open up, this could be of particular significance, since Japan has a capacity to provide many of the capital goods needed by China, and could use some of the commodities now being exported by the Chinese to the Soviet Union.

Any equation for predicting the future contains so many unknowns and variables that prediction is hazardous. It seems highly probable, however, that Communist China's economy and industrial base will continue to grow at a comparatively rapid pace; that the Chinese Communists will continue to promote trade relations with the free world and particularly with underdeveloped countries in Asia, the Middle East,and Africa; that Peking's foreign aid programs to countries in the Asian-African area may well be expanded in the years immediately ahead; and that the psychological impact of Communist China's economic developmnt will be widely felt throughout the underdeveloped areas of the world. All of these trends will be important factors in the economic competition between the entire Communist bloc and the West. There can be no doubt that Communist China's domestic economic development and foreign economic policies present a serious challenge to the free world, a challenge which the West cannot fail to take into consideration in formulating economic policies for the future.

APPENDIX

Note on Sources, Statistics, and Currency Conversion

The basic research material for this study has consisted of Chinese Communist official publications, principally newspapers and magazines. The most useful translated material is contained in Survey of the China Mainland Press (SCMP), Extracts from China Mainland Magazines (ECMM), and the Current Background (CB) Series of major Chinese Communist documents, all of which are issued by the American Consulate General in Hong Kong. A large percentage of the items in these publications is from the Peking People's Daily and the daily releases of the New China News Agency. Statistics on the Chinese Communist economy have been drawn principally from these sources. In addition, however, publications of the United States Department of Commerce, including its Value Series and Country-by-Commodity Series of statistical sheets, have provided data on trade between free world areas and Communist China.

Footnotes giving sources for all the detailed data in the study have been avoided in the text, but the documented tables in the Appendix give specific references on sources for some of the most important statistical data.

Although much of the available information on the Chinese Communist economy must be gleaned in fragmentary form from scattered reports, speeches, and articles, there are a few major reports on economic matters made by Chinese Communist leaders which are of particular importance. The following list includes several which have been the sources for many of the data included in the statistical tables. In the statistical tables they will be referred to simply by the names of the persons giving the report and the date of the report, or in other abbreviated forms.

The major source for statistics on the Chinese Communist economy up through the year 1955, are the tables accompanying the Communique on the Fulfillment of the Economic Plan for 1955, which was released by the State Statistical Bureau on June 14, 1956. (CB 429, November 26, 1956.) (Hereafter, Communique 1955.)

The most important source for the targets of the first Five Year Plan as of the time they were first announced in mid-1955 is the Report on the First Five Year Plan for the Development of the National Economy, a speech made by Li Fu-chun, Vice Premier and Chairman of the State Planning Commission, to the National People's Congress (NPC) on July 5-6, 1955. (New China News Agency, July 9, 1955.)

Among the most important sources for statistical and other economic data during 1956 and 1957 are:

Report on the Second Five Year Plan, by Premier Chou En-lai to the 8th National Congress of the Chinese Communist Party on September 16, 1956. (CB 413, October 5, 1956.)

Proposals on the Second Five Year Plan for the Development of the National Economy, adopted by the party Congress on September 27, 1956. (CB 413, October 5, 1956) (Hereafter, Proposals Second Plan.)

Report on the Work of the Government, by Chou En-lai to the NPC on June 26, 1957. (CB 463, July 2, 1957.)

Final Accounts for 1956 and the 1957 State Budget, delivered by Minister of Finance, Li Hsien-nien to the NPC on July 29, 1957. (CB 464, July 5, 1957.)

Working of the National Economic Plan for 1956 and Draft National Economic Plan for 1957, report by Po Yi-po, Vice Premier and Chairman of the National Economic Commission, to the NPC on July 1, 1957. (CB 465, July 9, 1957.)

Communique on the Fulfillment of the National Economic Plan for 1956, issued by the State Statistical Bureau on August 1, 1957. (CB 474, August 12, 1957.) (Hereafter, Communique 1956.)

The Foreign Trade of China, a report by Minister of Foreign Trade, Yeh Chi-Chuang to the NPC on July 11, 1957. (CB 468, July 22, 1957.)

Principles for 1958 Economic Plan Outlined by Po Yi-po, a press summary of a report by Po Yi-po to a party cadre meeting on August 10, 1957. (SCMP 1602, September 3, 1957.)

Draft Plan for Development of the National Economy in 1958, a report by Po Yi-po to the NPC on February 3, 1958. (CB 494, February 19, 1958.)

The Implementation of the State Budget for 1957 and the Draft State Budget for 1958, a report by Li Hsien-nien to the NPC on February 1, 1958. (CB 493, February 17, 1958.)

The necessity of relying primarily upon official Communist sources for statistical data creates obvious problems and limitations, in view of Communist manipulation of statistics for propaganda purposes. Nonetheless, these are the only data available, and if subjected to careful analysis, they reveal the basic aspects of existing economic conditions, even if many specific figures remain open to question. In this connection, attention is drawn to the Annex to Chapter Two.

A number of revisions and recomputations of national income aggregates by Western methods are now in progress. Information drawn from William W. Hollister, China's Gross National Product and Social Accounts 1950-1957, The Free Press, Glencoe, Illinois, 1958, is included in Appendix Table 1.

All Chinese monetary figures have been converted to U.S. dollars. The exchange rate used in the conversion has in all cases been the Chinese Communist official rate of $1.00 = 2.367 yuan. This is an artificial rate, since there is no free exchange of these currencies, and it undoubtedly exaggerates the value of Chinese Communist currency in international trade somewhat, although the distortion may not be too great. Some figures have been converted from rubles to dollars at the official rate of $1.00 = 4.00 rubles; the distortion involved in this conversion is probably considerably greater. However, the U.S. dollar figures have been used because they have more meaning than the original figures for American readers.

General Economic Indicators, 1952-1957
(billion dollars, except population and per capita figures;
current values, unless otherwise specified)

	1952	1953	1954	1955	1956	1957
Population	569	581	595	608	621	634
Communist data, unadjusted						
Total gross output (agricultural and industrial)	35.0	40.0	43.7	46.6	54.4	n.a.
Gross agricultural output	20.4	21.1	21.8	23.5	24.6	25.5
Gross industrial output	11.4	15.0	17.5	18.9	24.8	26.5
Gross handicraft output	3.1	3.9	4.4	4.3	5.0	n.a.
Capital goods output	4.5	6.2	7.4	8.7	12.3	13.9
Consumer goods output	6.9	8.8	10.1	10.2	12.5	12.7
State revenue	7.42	9.10	11.08	11.49	12.14	12.97
State expenditures	7.09	9.04	11.66	12.40	12.92	12.91
Capital construction expenditures a/	1.57	2.75	3.18	3.65	5.91	5.23
National income, current prices	-	30.6	32.7	34.6	38.6	41.5
National income, 1952 prices	25.8	29.6	31.2	33.3	37.5	39.5
National income, 1952 prices, per capita, dollars	45.4	50.9	52.4	54.8	60.3	62.3
Communist data, recomputed according to						
U. S. Department of Commerce concept (1952 prices)						
Gross national product	28.67	32.56	34.61	36.09	41.07	43.27
Gross national product per capita, dollars	50.39	55.85	58.17	59.36	66.14	68.25
Gross domestic investment	4.26	5.47	6.61	6.50	7.87	10.34
Consumption	24.80	27.37	28.16	29.94	33.27	32.92
Personal consumption	21.45	23.35	24.15	25.87	29.03	29.03
Personal consumption per capita, dollars	37.70	40.05	40.59	42.55	46.75	45.79

a/ For an explanation of "capital construction," see footnote 2, page 102.

Notes and Sources:

The official Chinese Communist census figure for 1953 was 583 million. The figures used in this table for the years 1952-56 are official Chinese estimates as of mid-year each year. The 1957 figure is an independent estimate based on past figures and the official figure on rate of growth. If one estimated year-end population figures, they would be approximately 575 million in 1952 and 640 million in 1957.

Total output, agricultural output, industrial output, capital goods output, and consumer goods output figures are from the following sources: 1952-55, Communique 1955; 1956, Po Yi-po July 1957; 1957, Po Yi-po February 1958. Agricultural output figures include subsidiary occupations. The figures for gross industrial output exclude the output of individual handicrafts, figures for which are given separately.

State revenue and expenditure figures are from official Chinese Communist budget statements. The official budget reports include those by Li Hsien-nien on February 1, 1958, June 29, 1957, June 15, 1956, and July 6, 1955; that by Teng Hsiao-ping on June 16, 1954; and that by Po Yi-po on February 13, 1953. Texts of these reports are available in CB and SCMP as well as in the New China News Agency releases.

National income figures are computed from Chinese Communist published figures in percentage form.

Figures for 1953-56 in current prices are derived from data in Peking Review, No. 6, April 8, 1958, giving military and administrative expenditures both as percentages of state expenditures and as percentages of national income. However, it appears that the figures given there for 1953 include most of the item "miscellaneous expenditures," so that the national income figure for 1953 is derived by applying the percentage given against the figure for total budget expenditures for that year. The figure for 1957 is derived from a statement in ECMM No. 136, July 21, 1958, that total national income for 1953-57 in current prices was 421.4 billion yuan or $178.03 billion.

(The difficulty of working with available Chinese Communist statistics is illustrated by the fact that a somewhat different set of figures for national income in current prices during 1952-56 can be derived from another set of percentages giving state revenue and capital construction as percentages of national income; these are in SCMP 1510, April 15, 1957. The figures derived from these percentages would be (in $ bill.): 1952-26.86, 1953-31.51, 1954-34.11, 1955-36.01, 1956-38.61. The figures used in the table are more recent, however, and appear to be more usable.)

The figures on national income for 1952-56 in constant 1952 prices are also derived from percentages given in the Peking Review cited above. The figure for 1957 is derived from a reported increase of 53 percent over 1952, in ECMM No. 132, June 16, 1958.

Capital construction figures come from Communique 1955, Chou En-lai, June 1957, Li Hsien-nien, July 1957, and Po Yi-po, July 1957, Li Hsien-nien, February 1958, and Po Yi-po, February 1958.

Communist data, recomputed according to U.S. Department of Commerce concepts by William W. Hollister, op. cit., pp. 132-3. See also text Table 2 in the present study and the accompanying discussion.

Appendix Table 2

First Five Year Plan: Targets and Claimed Achievements;
Second Five Year Plan Targets
(percentage increases)

	1st Plan target 1957 over 1952	Claimed 1st Plan achievement 1957 over 1952	Preliminary 2nd Plan target 1962 over 1st Plan target
National income	n.a.	54	about 50
Per capita national income	n.a.	38	n.a.
Gross output-agriculture and industry	51.1	64	70 to 75
Gross agricultural output	23.3	24.7	35
Gross industrial output	98.3	118.9	about 100
Grain output	17.6	19	n.a.
Modern industry output	104.1	132.5	n.a.
Capital goods output	126.5	204.3	n.a.
Consumer goods output	79.7	85.1	n.a.
Increase in workers' wages	33	37	n.a.

Sources: 1st Plan Target figures are from Li Fu-chun, July, 1956.

1st Plan Achievement figures are from Chou En-lai, Proposals 2nd Plan, September 1956. Proposals 2nd Plan, Po Yi-po, August 1957, and Po Yi-po, February 1958.

Preliminary 2nd Plan Target figures are from same sources as above, especially Chou En-lai, September 1956, and Proposals 2nd Plan.

Grain output figures include soya beans. If soya beans are excluded, the figures would be 23.6 for 1st Plan Target and 19.8 percent for Claimed 1st Plan Achievement. Gross industrial output figures exclude individual handicraft output, except for the 2nd Plan Target which probably includes handicrafts.

Gross agricultural output figures include subsidiary occupations.

Appendix Table 3

First Five Year Plan--Overall Capital Construction Plan
(covering entire five year period)

	$ billion	% of total
All capital construction	18.06	100.0
Industry	10.49	58.2
Transportation and communications	3.47	19.2
Agriculture, forestry and water conservancy	1.38	7.6
Education, health and culture	1.30	7.2
Municipal utilities	.68	3.7
Banking, trade, stockpiling	.54	3.0
Other	.19	1.1

Source: Li Fu-chun, July 1955.

Appendix Table 4

First Five Year Plan -- Capital Construction in Industry and Agriculture Compared to Totals
(billion dollars)

	Planned for 1953-57 period	Actual 1953	Actual 1954	Actual 1955	Actual 1956	Actual 1957	Claimed actual total for 1953-57 period
All capital construction	18.06	2.75	3.17	3.65	5.91	5.23	20.71
Industry	10.49	1.16	1.54	1.78	2.90	2.77	10.15
Agriculture, forestry and water conservancy	1.38	.28	.15	.25	.49	about .89	about 2.06

Sources: Figures on plans for 1953-57 are from Li Fu-chun, July 1955.

Figures on 1953-55 are from Communique 1955.

Figures on 1956 are from Chou En-lai, June 1957, Po Yi-po, July 1957, Li Hsien-nien, July 1957.

Figures on 1957, except for the figure for agriculture, are from Li Hsien-nien, February 1958, and Po Yi-po, February 1958.

The figure on agriculture for 1957 is derived. China Reconstructs of May 1958 states that planned capital construction for 1958 in this field is $1.24 billion and that this is about 40 percent above the 1957 figure, indicating a 1957 figure of about $.89 billion.

All totals for the 1953-57 period are the sum of individual figures for the five years. Po Yi-po, February 1958, gives a five year total of $20.61 billion for all capital construction, which differs slightly from the total derived by adding the individual figures for all five years.

Appendix Table 5

Industrial Output—Selected Items
(units — see each item)

	Pre-1949 peak (and year)	1949	1952	1st Plan target for 1957	Claimed 1957 output	Preliminary 2nd Plan target for 1962
Steel (mill. tons)	.923 (1943)	.158	1.35	4.12	5.35	10.5-12
Pig iron (mill. tons)	1.80 (1943)	.246	1.9	4.67	5.9	n.a.
Electric power production (bill. kwh)	5.96 (1941)	4.31	7.26	15.9	19.03	40-43
Coal (mill. tons)	61.88 (1942)	30.98	63.53	112.99	128.62	190-210
Crude oil (mill. tons)	.320(1943)	.122	.436	2.01	1.46	5-6
Cement (mill. tons)	2.29 (1942)	.661	2.86	6.0	6.69	12.5-14.5
Sulphate of ammonia (mill. tons)	.227(1941)	.027	.181	.578	.755	3.0-3.2
Metal cutting machine tools (thousand sets)	5.4 (1941)	1.8	13.7	12.7	22.64	60-65
Trucks (number)	0	0	0	4,000	10,000	n.a.
Cotton yarn (mill. bales)	2.45 (1933)	1.80	3.62	5.0	4.61	8-9
Cotton piece goods (mill. bolts)	n.a.	n.a.	111.63	163.72	149.91	235-260
Salt (mill. tons)	3.92 (1943)	n.a.	4.95	7.55	n.a.	10-11
Sugar (including handmade) (mill. tons)	.414(1936)	n.a.	.451	1.1	.874	2.4-2.5
Machine-made paper (mill. tons)	.165(1943)	.108	.372	.655	n.a.	1.5-1.6

Sources: All pre-1949, 1949 and 1952 figures (except for salt, sugar, and cotton piece goods) are from Communique 1955. For these years, salt and sugar figures are from Proposals 2nd Plan. For cotton piece goods, 1952 figure is from Li Fu-chun, July 1955.

1st and 2nd Plan target figures are from Li Fu-chun, July 1955, Po Yi-po, July 1957, Proposals 2nd Plan. The target for machine tool output for 1957 seems unreasonable on the surface, because of a seeming drop compared to 1952, but actually a large increase in tonnage output of machine tools was involved.

The 1957 figures (claimed output) come from the following sources:

Coal, electric power, cement, machine tools, and sulphate of ammonia figures come from China Reconstructs, April 1958 (vol. VII, No. 4). The figure for sulphate of ammonia includes all nitrogenous and phosphate chemical fertilizers.

Steel figure from NCNA, September 14, 1958.

Pig iron, cotton yarn, and trucks figures come from People's Daily, January 1, 1958. The figure for trucks includes all motor vehicles.

The figure for crude oil is derived. The 1958 oil output target in Communist China is 1.55 million tons, and this is said to be 6.2 percent above 1957 output, indicating a 1957 output of 1.46 million tons.

The figures for cotton piece goods and sugar are mid-1957 estimates of the year's production rather than final claims. The former comes from Li Hsien-nien, July 1957 and the latter from Po Yi-po, July 1957.

Not all figures published by the Chinese Communists on 1957 production coincide with the ones used in this table. The following are a few of the contradictory statistics on 1957 output: steel - 5.24 million (China Reconstructs, April 1958); electricity - 18.99 billion kwh (People's Daily, January 1, 1958); coal - 130 million (NCNA, September 14, 1958); cement - 6.8 million (People's Daily, January 1, 1958); chemical fertilizers - 800,000 tons (NCNA, March 11, 1958).

Notes: The above figures for pre-1949 peaks differ in some instances considerably from non-Communist estimates.

Figures on cotton piece goods output for pre-1949 and 1949 are available but have been omitted as not being comparable with later statistics. The Communists state that the pre-1949 output was 45 million bolts, but this figure includes only production of modern industry and handicraft workshops. The piece goods figures in this table include individual handicraft output of cloth which is wholly or in part made of machine-made yarn. The yarn figures here do not include yarn made by individual handicraftsmen, however.

Appendix Table 6

Agricultural Production—Grain and Cotton
(million tons)

	Pre-1949 peak (and year)	1952	1st Plan 1957 target	Claimed output 1957	Claimed output 1958	Preliminary 2nd Plan 1962 target
Grain	138.7 (1936)	163.9	192.8	185(195)	375	250
Cotton	.849 (1936)	1.304	1.635	1.64	3.32	2.4

Sources: Pre-1949 figures are from Proposals 2nd Plan.

1952 figures are from Communique 1955.

1st Plan target figures are from Li Fu-chun, July 1955.

The 1957 grain and cotton figures come from Po Yi-po, February, 1958. The 1958 claimed output was reported in a Reuters news dispatch from Hong Kong, April 14, 1959, which refers to a "communique from the State Statistical Bureau, quoted by the New China News Agency."

2nd Plan targets are from Proposals 2nd Plan.

Note: Grain figures include soya beans and potatoes, as well as grain. The 1957 output of grain and tubers alone, not counting soya bean production, was 185 million tons; soya bean production was reported to be 9.8 million tons; therefore the total is 195 million tons.

Appendix Table 7

Estimated Balance of Payments 1953-1957
(million dollars)

(R=receipts; O=outpayments)

	1953-54 (2 year Period) a/		1955		1956		1957		Total 1953-57	
	R	O	R	O	R	O	R	O	R	O
Trade	3,195	3,817	2,096	2,561	2,352	2,238	2,280	2,019	9,923	10,635
Soviet credits and Chinese repayments	558	26	700	203	50	260	10	274	1,318	763
Chinese foreign aid	-	118	-	166	-	171	-	192	-	647
Other	208	-	134	-	267	-	195	-	804	-
Total	3,961	3,961	2,930	2,930	2,669	2,669	2,485	2,485	12,045	12,045

a/ The years 1953-54 are combined because it is not possible to break down into annual figures the available data on China's foreign aid for these two years.

Sources and Notes:

Figures on trade: See Appendix Table 8.

Figures on foreign credits and loans to China (and it is presumed all foreign loans are Soviet loans) for 1956-57 are from Li Hsien-nien, July 1957. The figure for 1957 was the planned target. Final accounts for 1957 did not have a specific figure on actual deliveries.

Figures on Soviet credits and loans to China for 1953-55 are derived as follows: Budget data for these years give figures for total receipts and breakdown of domestic receipts other than foreign aid. The unaccounted-for receipts represent foreign aid. (See Appendix Table 1 reference for official budget statements.) The above 1953-54 figure combines the following annual figures: 1953 - $185 million, 1954 - $373 million.

Figures on Chinese servicing and repayments of Soviet aid for 1955-57 are derived as follows: Budgets for these years include figures on total debt servicing, including both domestic and foreign debts, which are $281 million in 1955, $305 million in 1956, and $354 million in 1957. It is estimated that servicing charges on the domestic debt, including all known bond issues, amounted to $78 million in 1955, $45 million in 1956, and $80 million in 1957. By subtracting domestic debt carrying charges from total debt carrying charges, estimates can be obtained on servicing and repayments of Soviet loans.

Figures on Chinese servicing and repayments of Soviet aid for 1953-54 are derived as follows: 1953 budget

includes a figure of $711 million for "other expenditures," including all debt servicing, China's own foreign aid, and other unspecified expenditures. The 1954 budget includes a figure of $267 million for the same category, but in addition specifies that $88 million of this is for debt servicing. From these figures, and all available fragmentary data on the domestic debt, past Soviet loans, and other miscellaneous expenditures it is possible to arrive at a rough estimate of the expenditures for servicing Soviet loans during those years.

Figures for China's foreign aid expenditures in 1956 and 1957 are from Li Hsien-nien, July 1957, and Li Hsien-nien, February 1958.

Figures for China's foreign aid expenditures in 1953-55 are estimates derived from computations described above (in relation to servicing and repaying Soviet loans) plus data published on actual deliveries of Chinese aid to North Korea during this period.

The item "other" is computed as the difference between known outpayments and known receipts. Its composition by invisible categories, changes in reserves and gold, overseas remittances, etc. is not known. Remittances from overseas Chinese are a major item. This table assumes that there has been no change in Communist China's foreign exchange reserves during this period. In actual fact, Peking collected significant quantities of foreign currency and gold from the population during 1951-52, and these may have been utilized during this period. If this took place, the estimates for "other" in the table should be lower.

97

Appendix Table 8

Estimated Foreign Trade 1950-57 (Chinese Communist Sources)
(million dollars)

	Total trade	Imports	Exports	Trade balance	Communist bloc trade	Free world trade
1950	1,757	896	861	− 35	589	1,168
1951	2,513	1,483	1,030	−453	1,590	923
1952	2,741	1,590	1,151	−439	2,140	601
1953	3,427	1,953	1,474	−479	2,587	840
1954	3,585	1,864	1,721	−143	2,888	697
1955	4,657	2,561	2,096	−465	3,819	838
1956	4,590	2,238	2,352	+114	3,456	1,134
1957	4,299	2,019	2,280	+261	n.a.	n.a.
Total for 1953-57	20,558	10,635	9,923	−712	n.a.	n.a.

Note: Vneshnyaya Torgovlya, No. 11, November 1957, published some figures on China-USSR trade alone which indicate a trade level in 1956 of $1,497 million; using published percentages on the relative value of Soviet and Satellite trade, this would indicate that total Communist China-Communist bloc trade in 1956 was $2.25 billion. The Chinese newspaper Ta Kung Pao on January 1, 1958 (SCMP 1704) published ruble figures on China-USSR trade which placed the 1956 level at the equivalent of $1,747 million, indicating a total Communist China-Communist bloc trade of $2.68 billion. It is impossible to reconcile such differences or to know with certainty why these figures are lower than those used in the above table. Probably the ruble figures exclude some important items in Sino-Soviet trade, in particular Soviet exports of military equipment. Possibly, discrepencies may arise from the difficulty of converting both Russian ruble and Chinese yuan figures into dollars at official exchange rates when in fact the figures represent barter transactions and little is known of pricing arrangements. Soviet statistics for 1957 indicate that Sino-Soviet trade in that year dropped to $1.28 billion. Chinese sources estimated it would increase in 1958 to a level of perhaps $1.5 billion. (Harry Schwartz, The New York Times, November 8, 1958.)

Sources: Figures on total trade and total imports and exports for 1957 come from Peking Review, June 17, 1958. See also article by Shigeyoshi Takami on "Prospects for Trade with Continental China" in Contemporary Japan, April 1958.

Figures on total trade and total imports and exports for 1956 come from Yeh Chi-chuang, July 1957. The figure for total trade for 1954 comes from Foreign Trade of the People's Republic of China, China Committee for the Promotion of International Trade, Peking, 1956. All other figures on total trade and imports and exports are derived by using indices covering several years. The sources of these indices are: Trade with China, A Practical Guide, Ta Kung Pao, Hong Kong, 1957, (includes 1950-55 index); Asia Keizi: Junpo, Tokyo, March 1, 1957 (includes index of total trade, imports and exports 1950-55 from Canton Trade Fair data); and China Reconstructs, September 1956 (1950-55 index).

The figures on Soviet bloc and free world trade are derived by taking the figures on total trade and applying to them percentages of China trade which has been with the Soviet bloc or with the free world each year. The most detailed set of percentages of this sort are in Soviet publications: Vneshnyaya Torgovlya, No. 5, 1956, Moscow; and Razvitie Ekonomiki Stran Narodnoi Demokratii Asii, Moscow, 1956.

Appendix Table 9

Mainland China's Free-World Trade Turnover, Selected Years 1948-1957,
By Selected Trading Partners (U. S. Department of Commerce Data)
(million dollars)

	1948	1950	1952	1954	1956	1957	1958
Hong Kong	179.1	405.8	236.3	189.5	205.5	219.5	271.8
Japan	28.9	59.0	15.5	59.9	151.0	141.0	105.0
Ceylon	0.9	0.6	32.8	78.6	66.4	52.8	48.2
Malaya	56.7	71.8	39.5	34.8	50.8	76.4	101.9
India	27.1	6.2	44.2	13.5	33.1	19.5	18.3
Egypt	0.8	4.4	9.6	12.2	35.4	62.7	42.3
Morocco	9.2	10.7	5.5	11.2	19.8	12.5	19.1
West Germany	4.3	26.0	20.4	57.6	90.2	88.8	220.9
United Kingdom	65.2	39.0	21.3	44.6	65.4	74.0	128.2
France	11.4	8.7	8.8	18.1	37.5	34.5	55.7
Above 10 countries	383.6	632.2	433.9	520.0	755.1	781.7	1,011.4
All other	639.0	354.6	203.7	136.2	299.2	360.8	456.9
Total	1,022.6	986.8	637.6	656.2	1,054.3	1,142.5	1,468.3
Listed 10 countries as percent of total free world	37.5	64.1	68.1	79.2	71.6	68.4	68.9

Source: U.S. Department of Commerce trade sheets, Value Series and Country-by-Commodity Series.

Notes: A major omission in this table is Switzerland, whose trade with China was listed as $54.37 million in 1956 and has exceeded $30 million every year since 1950 with one exception. It has been excluded from this table, however, because the statistics on Switzerland include trade with Hong Kong and Macao (as well as Outer Mongolia in 1948 and Formosa in 1950–52). Actually a large percentage of the figures for Switzerland consist of Hong Kong trade, and there is no way to estimate trade with Communist China from these figures. Switzerland is, however, one of the largest European traders with China and perhaps should rank after West Germany and the United Kingdom.

The figures above on several other countries also include areas other than Communist China, since their governments use different formulae for compiling their statistics and the U.S. Commerce Department merely reproduces them as received; but in no cases other than Switzerland does this fact radically distort the general picture of their trade with Communist China. The figures on the following countries include areas other than Communist China:

Ceylon includes Formosa, Outer Mongolia and North Korea
Egypt includes Outer Mongolia and North Korea
France includes Formosa
Morocco includes Formosa (1948–51)
Germany includes Formosa and Outer Mongolia
Hong Kong includes Formosa.

The reporting period varies for different countries also.

All of these figures are therefore unadjusted statistics, and although the totals can be assumed to represent an approximate indication of trade with Communist China, these statistics are not always exact figures on Communist China's trade with some of the countries listed.

NOTES

Chapter Two

1. Throughout this study all Chinese Communist figures in Yuan have been converted to United States dollars at the official rate of US $1.00 = Yuan 2.367. This is an artificial rate, and it undoubtedly exaggerates the value of Chinese Communist currency in international trade somewhat (see Appendix). Some figures used in this study have been converted from rubles to dollars at the official rate of $1.00 = 4.00 Rubles; the distortion involved in this conversion is probably still greater. Nonetheless, for the use of Western readers dollar figures seem preferable to the original Yuan or Ruble figures.

2. "Capital construction" is a budgetary term and refers to the government's fixed capital expenditures, whether for economic, social, military, or administrative purposes. It includes expenditures for the repair and replacement of capital assets.

3. "Above-norm" construction projects are those requiring cabinet-level approval and involving new investments exceeding certain arbitrary "investment norms" which vary from $1.25 million for projects in some light industries to $4.22 million for projects in heavy industries, such as iron and steel.

4. See William W. Hollister, China's Gross National Product and Social Accounts, 1950-1957, The Free Press, Glencoe, Illinois, 1958; and T. C. Liu, "Structural Changes in the Economy on the Chinese Mainland, 1933 and 1952-57," Papers and Proceedings, American Economic Review, May, 1958. Hollister's and Liu's conclusions are based upon extensive and detailed calculations, and hence are used in this analysis in preference to estimates of growth based upon the Chinese national income figures. As explained in the notes to Appendix Table 1, on the basis of available data it is possible to arrive at more than one series of statistics on China's national income during 1952-57. However, if the series actually used in Appendix Table 1 were accepted, it would suggest an annual rate of growth in the national income (in constant prices) of 8.6 percent.

5. Hollister, op. cit., p. XVIII.

6. Hollister, op. cit., p. 6.

7. Wilfred Malenbaum, loc. cit.

8. See Table 2. See also Hollister, op. cit., pp. 6, 13, 133.

9. Ibid., p. 6.

10. These percentages were calculated as increases by 1962 over the first Five Year Plan's 1957 targets rather than over actual 1957 output.

Annex to Chapter Two

11. For a discussion of the principal sources used, see the Appendix "Note on Sources, Statistics, and Currency Conversion."

Chapter Four

1. The term "aid project" as used by the Chinese and Russians implies technical assistance and supply commitments, but not necessarily financial aid.

Notes to Chapter Four, Continued

2. Satellite economic assistance to China is discussed in Jan Wszelaki, Communist Economic Strategy: The Role of East-Central Europe, National Planning Association, Washington, D. C., January 1959, the first study of a series of NPA special project reports on The Economics of Competitive Coexistence.

Chapter Five

1. The Chinese Communists initially reported soya beans with grains, but later separated the two; this presents problems in evaluating their grain figures.

Chapter Seven

1. These were actually signs of a drop in Communist China's exports to non-Communist countries in early 1959, and it is difficult to reconcile this with Peking's claims of economic progress.

Chapter Eight

1. Since the Chinese Communists have not published detailed, general statistics on trade, many of the figures used throughout this section are estimates. See Appendix Table 8 for sources and bases for these estimates.
2. See Jan Wszelaki, op. cit., Chapter Ten.
3. However, some of China's exports of rice to Southeast Asia may have really been re-exports of Burmese rice; in 1954 and 1955, the Chinese contracted to purchase 150,000 tons of rice a year from Burma.

Chapter Nine

1. These unadjusted figures, taken from U.S. Department of Commerce Value Series on free world trade with the Sino-Soviet bloc, do not take account in their trade statistics of lags in reporting by various countries, costs of freight and insurance in China's imports, and double-counting of certain Chinese exports to free world areas, or of the fact that some free world areas combine Mainland China with Mongolia, Formosa, and, in a few cases, even Hong Kong and Macao. If adjusted to take account of all of these factors, Department of Commerce statistics might indicate a level of perhaps $940 million in 1956. See Appendix Tables 8 and 9.
2. The subject of Japanese-Chinese trade is discussed fully in H. Michael Sapir, Japan, China, and the West, a study in the series on The Economics of Competitive Coexistence, National Planning Association, Washington, D. C., 1959.
3. See Sapir, op. cit., Chapter Nine.

Conclusion

1. One indication of this is the fact that the overall additional industrial capacity which Japanese economic projections envisage for the next five years is probably larger than Communist China's total industrial capacity.
2. See New Long-Range Economic Plan of Japan (FY 1958-FY 1962), Economic Planning Agency, Japanese Government, Tokyo, 1958, p. 87.

Research Staff of the NPA Project on
THE ECONOMICS OF COMPETITIVE COEXISTENCE

National Planning Association Staff

Gerhard Colm, Chief Economist, NPA

Project Research Staff

Henry G. Aubrey, Director of Research
Sidney Schmukler, Associate Director of Research*
Joel Darmstadter, Research Associate
Stella P. Jablonski, Secretary

Consultants

A. Doak Barnett, Council on Foreign Relations, New York City
Peter G. Franck, Robert College, Istanbul, Turkey
Alec Nove, London University, London, England
H. Michael Sapir, U.N. Technical Assistance Administration, Santiago, Chile
Wolfgang F. Stolper, University of Michigan, Ann Arbor, Michigan
Paul Wohl, Economic Consultant and Writer, New York City
Jan Wszelaki, Economic Consultant and Writer, Washington, D. C.

Research Contracts

Center for International Studies, Massachusetts Institute of Technology, Cambridge, Massachusetts (Wilfred Malenbaum)

---

*Until November, 1957.

NPA PUBLICATIONS POLICY

NPA is an independent, nonpolitical, nonprofit organization established in 1934. It is an organization where leaders of agriculture, business, labor, and the professions join in programs to maintain and strengthen private initiative and enterprise.

Those who participate in the activities of NPA believe that the tendency to break up into pressure groups is one of the gravest disintegrating forces in our national life. America's number-one problem is that of getting diverse groups to work together for this objective: To combine our efforts to the end that the American people may always have the highest possible cultural and material standard of living without sacrificing our freedom. Only through joint democratic efforts can programs be devised which support and sustain each other in the national interest.

NPA's Standing Committees—the Agriculture, Business, and Labor Committees on National Policy and the Committee on International Policy—and its Special Committees are assisted by a permanent research staff. Whatever their particular interests, members have in common a fact-finding and socially responsible attitude.

NPA believes that through effective private planning we can avoid a "planned economy." The results of NPA's work will not be a grand solution to all our ills. But the findings, and the process of work itself, will provide concrete programs for action on specific problems, planned in the best traditions of a functioning democracy.

NPA's publications—whether signed by its Board, its Committees, its staff, or by individuals—are issued in an effort to pool different knowledges and skills, to narrow areas of controversy, and to broaden areas of agreement.

All reports published by NPA have been examined and authorized for publication under policies laid down by the Board of Trustees. Such action does not imply agreement by NPA Board or Committee members with all that is contained therein, unless such endorsement is specifically stated.

NATIONAL PLANNING ASSOCIATION

A Voluntary Association Incorporated under the Laws of the District of Columbia
1606 NEW HAMPSHIRE AVE., N. W., WASHINGTON 9, D. C.
JOHN MILLER: *Assistant Chairman* and *Executive Secretary*
EUGENE H. BLAND: *Editor of Publications*